Living by Faith

E. J. Waggoner

A. T. Jones

"And he shewed me a pure river of water of life, clear as crystal, proceeding out of the throne of God and of the Lamb. And the Spirit and the bride say, Come. And let him that heareth say, Come. And let him that is athirst come. And whosoever will, let him take the water of life freely." Rev. 22:1,17.

Will you?

Living by Faith
>A companion book to *Lessons on Faith*.

Contact
>www.LivingByFaithBook.com
>LivingByFaithBook@gmail.com

Published by
>Nora Roth
>2641 Seminary Hill Rd
>Centralia, WA 98531

Editors
>Nora Roth
>Julie Roth

Acknowledgments
>Larry Roth, my husband, for creative and technical help.
>Julie Roth, my daughter, for editing and suggestions.
>Elora Ford, Bob Ford, and Mary Lou Steinweg, my
>mother, brother, and sister, for ideas and encouragement.
>
>Cover photo by Nora Roth.

Published in 2014

Available from www.LivingByFaithBook.com

ISBN-13: 978-1495229503

Scriptures from the King James Version of the Bible, unless
otherwise noted.

Foreword

Why is this book important? I believe that very soon we will come to the greatest time of trouble our world has ever experienced. Both the power of God and the power of the devil will be displayed. How can we be ready for this? The Lord has given a message to prepare us for this time and He will make a compelling appeal to each of us.

In the book of Revelation we read: *"And I saw another angel fly in the midst of heaven, having the everlasting gospel to preach to them that dwell on the earth, and to every nation, and kindred, and tongue, and people, saying with a loud voice, Fear God, and give glory to Him; for the hour of His judgment is come: and worship Him that made heaven, and earth, and the sea, and fountains of water."* Rev. 14:6,7.

What is this everlasting gospel? How do we prepare for the judgment? How do we give glory to God? How do we worship the Creator?

The best answers I have found come from a message the Lord gave through two ministers, Elders Waggoner and Jones. Their writings contain the clearest presentation of the gospel I have read.

"The Lord in His great mercy sent a most precious message to His people through Elders Waggoner and Jones. This message was to bring more prominently before the world the uplifted Saviour, the sacrifice for the sins of the whole world. It presented justification through faith in the Surety; it invited the people to receive the righteousness of Christ, which is made

3

manifest in obedience to all the commandments of God." Last Day Events by Ellen G. White, p. 200.

But this "most precious message" given through Elders Waggoner and Jones is not readily available. So this book brings together a selection of their writings containing the heart and soul of their message, presented in a way you can easily understand.

Because these articles were originally written in the late nineteenth century the language and style have been updated in places to make them more readable and more personal. The distinct presentation of the gospel remains unchanged.

God's purpose in giving you this message is so He can "make an end of sins" in your life; that through the faith of Jesus He can "bring in everlasting righteousness." Dan. 9:24. Then He will say of His people, "Here are they that keep the commandments of God, and the faith of Jesus." Rev. 14:12.

Nora Roth

Contents

~1~

The Keeping Power

The power that is able to save you is also able to keep you. When you believe, you "are kept by the power of God through faith unto salvation." 1 Peter 1:5. If your faith does not claim the power of God in the daily stress of sin it is not a saving faith. Whenever you fall into sin, it is because for that moment your faith has let go of the Lord, and you are not believing in Him.

For "whosoever believeth that Jesus is the Christ is born of God." Being born of God by faith is not something that is done once for all time, but is a continual process. It continues as long as you believe. And through faith you are kept by the power of God. "We know that whosoever is begotten of God sinneth not; but He that is begotten of God keepeth him, and the evil one toucheth him not." 1 John 5:18, R.V.

It is a blessed truth that through faith you are shut in by the arms of the Lord, and the evil one cannot touch you. There is refuge, a haven from the storm. Oh, that you might learn to abide in the shelter; for you know well enough by bitter experience that you do not have the power to keep yourself—not for even one moment.

Even in this world of sin and wickedness, through faith you can be kept from the iniquity that surrounds you, that is even in your very flesh ready to spring on you. When the three Hebrew captives were thrown into the furnace of fire, the fire had no power on their bodies, "nor was an hair of their head singed, neither were their coats changed, nor the smell of fire had passed on them." There was with them in the furnace One who had said,

"I will be with thee," and "when thou walkest through the fire, thou shalt not be burned."

It is He that is pledged to keep you in the midst of the consuming fire of sin. You cannot endure it alone; you always fall, and the fiery darts strike into your soul. The prayer of David may be yours continually, "Create in me a clean heart, O God; and renew a constant spirit [margin] within me." Thank God, when your faith has not held Him fast, and the enemy has found you and touched you, there is still the promise following the injunction, "sin not." "And if any man sin, we have an advocate with the Father, Jesus Christ the righteous." He releases you from the enemy and sets you free again. But He sets you free that you may hold steadfastly to Him by a firmer faith. In the bitterness of sin you are taught your own weakness and worthlessness, and in the sweetness of His forgiveness you are taught His power to save.

~2~

Light and Life

One of the characteristics of light is that it may multiply itself indefinitely without diminishing itself in the least. A lighted candle may give light to a million candles, and yet its own light is just as bright. The sun supplies light and heat to this earth, and there is enough for all. Each individual gets as much benefit from the sun now as it was possible for anyone to get when the population of the earth was only half as great as it is now. The sun gives its whole strength to each person, and yet it has as much heat and light as though it supplied no one.

Jesus Christ is the Sun of righteousness, and the Light of the world. The light which He gives is His life. "In Him was life, and the life was the light of men." John 1:4. He says, "He that followeth Me shall not walk in darkness, but shall have the light of life." John 8:12. He gives His life for the world. All who believe on Him receive His life, and are saved by it. Just as the light of the candle is not diminished although many others are lighted by it, so Christ's life is not diminished though He gives it to many. Every one of us may have it in all its fullness.

The light shone in the darkness, and the darkness could not overcome it. His light could not be quenched. Satan could not take His light, because he could not tempt Him to sin. Even when He laid down His life, He still had as much life left. His life triumphed over death. It is infinite life so He is able to save to the uttermost those who come to God by Him. Christ will dwell in His completeness in every one who will let Him. This is the mystery of the Gospel.

~3~

True Faith

One day a centurion came to Jesus, and said to Him: "Lord, my servant lieth at home sick of the palsy, grievously tormented. And Jesus saith unto him, I will come and heal him. The centurion answered and said, Lord, I am not worthy that Thou shouldest come under my roof; but speak the word only, and my servant shall be healed. ... When Jesus heard it, He marveled, and said to them that followed, Verily I say unto you, I have not found so great faith, no, not in Israel." Matt. 8:6-10.

Jesus pronounces this to be faith. When you find what that is, you have found faith. When you know what that is, you will know what faith is. There can be no doubt about this; for Christ is "the Author ... of faith," and He says that what the centurion manifested was "faith;" yes, even "great faith."

Where then, is the faith? The centurion wanted a certain thing done. He wanted the Lord to do it. But when the Lord said, "I will come" and do it, the centurion stopped him, saying, "Speak the word only," and it will be done.

Now, what did the centurion expect would do the work? "The word only." On what did he depend for the healing of his servant? "The word only."

And the Lord Jesus says that is faith.

Here was a Roman, despised and shunned as a heathen by Israel, and believed to be hated by God. He had spent his life among heathen influences, without the advantages of the Bible. Yet he had discovered that when the Lord speaks, in that word itself there is power to do what the word says, and he depended on that word to do what it said.

Then there were the people of Israel, who all their lives had been in daily connection with the word of the Lord, who prided themselves on being "the people of the Book," and boasted of their knowledge of the word of God; and yet they had not learned that in the word there is power to accomplish what the word says.

All their lives that word had plainly said to them: "As the rain cometh down, and the snow from heaven, and returneth not thither, but watereth the earth, and maketh it bring forth and bud, that it may give seed to the sower, and bread to the eater; so shall My word be that goeth forth out of My mouth; it shall not return unto Me void, but it shall accomplish that which I please, and it shall prosper in the thing whereto I sent it." Isa. 55:10, 11.

Nature itself held constantly before them the lesson that the earth of itself could produce nothing; that it was the moisture of rain and snow from heaven that made it bring forth and bud, and produce fruit.

And the Lord said, "So shall My word be." As the earth of itself can do nothing, so you of yourself can do nothing. And as the moisture of rain and snow from heaven makes the earth bring forth and bud, and produce fruit, so shall My word make you bring forth the fruit of righteousness to the glory of God. "My word, ... IT shall accomplish that which I please."

Many a time Israel had read this scripture. And year in and year out they had read the word of God, and had said: I will do what the word says; I will accomplish what pleases Him.

And that they might be certain that they should do exactly what the word said, they separated the word into parts, and each part was divided out into many fine distinctions. Then they set about to diligently, carefully and particularly, do each specification of the word, on their own.

True, nowhere in all this did they find any peace, much less any joy. With all their doing, they never found the things done. Always they found themselves far short of having done what the word said—so far short, that it was the despairing cry of Israel that "if but one person could only for one day keep the whole law, and not offend in one point—no, if but one person could but keep that one point of the law which affected the due observance of the Sabbath—then the troubles of Israel would be ended, and the Messiah would come at last." But they still slaved on in the treadmill round of their own fruitless doings—all of works, and none of faith; all of themselves, and none of God; all of their own doing, which was not really doing at all, and none of the word itself doing, which is the only real doing of the word of God.

How refreshing it was to the spirit of Jesus, in the midst of this desert waste of Israel, to meet a man who had found the word of God in truth; who knew that when the word was spoken, that the word itself would accomplish the thing spoken; and who would depend on "the word only." This was faith. This opened his life to the power of God. And the result was that there was accomplished in his life that which pleased God.

"My word, ... IT [not you] shall accomplish that which I please." "The word of God ... effectually worketh also in you that believe." 1 Thess. 2:13. To depend on it to work in you that which is well pleasing in His sight—this is faith. To cultivate this dependence on the word is to cultivate faith.

~4~

The Creative Word

The power of the word of God is best appreciated when you consider the work of creation. "By the word of the LORD were the heavens made; and all the host of them by the breath of His mouth. He gathereth the waters of the sea together as an heap; He layeth up the depth in storehouses. Let all the earth fear the LORD; let all the inhabitants of the world stand in awe of Him. For He spake, and it was *done*; He commanded, and it stood fast." Ps. 33:6-9.

From this it is plain to see that the entire material of the earth and all that is in it, sprang from the word of God. We cannot comprehend the power of Divinity, but we can see from what is plainly declared, that the word of the Lord is not empty air, but that it is real substance. It is as though the world existed in the word, before it took the shape that it's in now. When God's word was uttered, then the earth and the heavens came into existence.

When the word of God names something, then the thing that is named is formed. Whatever is described by the word, exists in that word. Thus it is impossible for God to lie, for His word makes the thing so. We read in Rom. 4:17 that God "calleth those things that be not as though they were." That is something that only God can do. It is true that we sometimes undertake it, but our word does not make the thing so. When you speak of a thing that is not as though it were, there is only one word that can be used to describe your action. It is a lie. But God cannot lie, yet He speaks of those things that do not exist as though they did. God speaks of something that has no existence. He calls it by name, as though it were well known. The instant that His word goes forth, that instant the thing exists.

Consider this text carefully. "He spake and it was." Not that He spake, and after that it was performed, as a superficial reading of the texts might lead you to think. That idea would not be gained if the translators had not inserted the word "done," in italics. It is true that it was done then, but it was the word of the Lord that did it. The idea would be conveyed better by translating the passage literally, as we have, "He spake, and it was." As soon as He spake, everything was there. Whatever God's word says, *is*, because His word creates the thing.

This is why in prophecy things are often spoken of as already done. He speaks of those things that haven't happened yet as though they were already done. This is not because they exist in His purpose, but because they exist in His word. They are as freely in existence as they can ever be, although they do not yet appear to human sight.

It is for this reason that the word of the Lord is strength and comfort to those who believe in it; for the word which is written in the Bible is the word of God, the same as that which created the heavens and the earth. "All scripture is given by inspiration of God." It is "God breathed." Now remember that "by the word of the Lord the heavens were made; and all the host of them by the breath of His mouth." The breath of God, which has creative energy in it, is that which gives us the precepts and promises of the Bible.

That creative word is the power of the Gospel. For the Gospel is the power of God unto salvation, to everyone that believes; and the power of God is revealed in the things that are made. See Rom. 1:16, 20. The power of redemption is the power of creation, for redemption is creation. Thus, the Psalmist prayed, "Create in me a clean heart, O God." Ps. 51:10. The apostle Paul says that "if any man be in Christ, he is a new creature." 2 Cor. 5:17.

What is this new creation that is brought about in the Gospel? It is righteousness, for the same apostle exhorted us to "put on the new man, which after God is created in righteousness and true holiness." Eph. 4:24. Righteousness means good works, and therefore the apostle says that "we are His workmanship, created in Christ Jesus unto good works, which God hath before ordained [or prepared] that we should walk in them." Eph. 2:10.

The word of the Lord is right. He speaks righteousness. So just as He spoke to emptiness and created the earth, so He speaks to the soul that is destitute of righteousness, and if that word is received, the righteousness of that word is on that person. "For all have sinned, and come short of the glory of God; being justified freely by His grace, through the redemption that is in Christ Jesus; whom God hath set forth to be a propitiation through faith in His blood, to declare His righteousness for the remission of sins that are passed, through the forbearance of God." Rom. 3:23-25. To declare is to speak; so when God declares His righteousness in Christ for the remission of sins, righteousness is spoken into and on you, to take the place of your sins, which are taken away. And it is not simply a passive righteousness that is declared on you, but real, active righteousness, for the word of the Lord is alive, and God's righteousness is real and active.

This, in brief, is what the story of creation means to you when you believe it. Satan is eager to have you think that it is only a poem (as though a poem could not be true), or only a writing of fiction to amuse you. This is the means which he has taken in these days to undermine the Gospel. If you once look lightly on creation, the force of the Gospel is weakened for you. Satan is even content that you should call redemption a greater work than that of creation, for by doing so you are not in the least exalting the work of redemption, but depreciating it. Redemption and creation are the same work, and redemption is exalted only as creation is greatly appreciated. It may occur to you that since this is the case, that which commemorates creation must also commemorate redemption. This is true, but we will speak of that at another time.

~5~

Weakness and Power

What is more frail, weak, and helpless than a little blade of grass? But did you ever notice the marvelous power that it exhibits?

Look at what is lifting that clod of dirt. It is a hard, heavy, impenetrable mass of dry clay. What is moving it so slowly and yet so surely out of its way? Not an animal, not even an insect—only a little blade of young grass! The clod is many times heavier than the grass, and yet the grass seems to lift it with the utmost ease. You could not cause a tiny grass root to exhibit such power. You might lay the clod on it ever so carefully but the grass would be crushed to the earth with the great weight of the clod. Some power that is not in the grass itself must be accomplishing this great wonder. The Bible says that it is the power and life of God's word that causes the grass to grow; for "God said, Let the earth bring forth grass: and it was so."

Look at a tiny acorn. How helpless, how worthless! But look again. An unseen life, a marvelous power, breaks the hard shell, and pushes little rootlets downward, and tiny branches upward. They grow and grow, turning aside hindrances, climbing over obstacles, and bursting asunder solid rocks. What is the unseen life? What is the marvelous power? The life and power of God's word; for "God said, Let the earth bring forth grass, the herb yielding seed, and the fruit-tree yielding fruit after his kind, whose seed is in itself upon the earth; and it was so."

Although they are two of the weakest and most helpless things in existence, yet what miracles of strength the grass and the acorn exhibit when their weakness is united to the power of

God's word. You are the same way. Weak? Yes, as weak and helpless as the grass. Your "days are as grass," "and all the glory of man as the flower of grass." Your life "even a vapor, that appeareth for a little time, and then vanisheth away." Helpless, utterly helpless in yourself, unable to care for yourself a single moment, unable to resist the smallest temptation, unable to do one good act.

But look again. An unseen power has taken possession of you, a new life has animated you, and lo, you have "subdued kingdoms, wrought righteousness, obtained promises, stopped the mouth of lions, quenched the violence of fire, escaped the edge of the sword, out of weakness were made strong, waxed valiant in fight, turned to flight the armies of the aliens!" Heb. 11:33, 34. While you were once weak, now you are strong; where once you would have trembled and fallen, now you stand unmoved like a house built on a solid rock.

What is this unseen power? What is your new life? It is the life and power of God's word united with your weakness. It is the life and power of God Himself, for God goes with His word "working in you that which is well pleasing in His sight." "For it is God which worketh in you both to will and to do of His good pleasure."

You alone, without the Word in you, are like a house that is built on the sand. There is nothing to hold you up when the floods come and the winds blow. It is utterly impossible for you to withstand the tempest, for you do not have strength in yourself.

But even if you are the most helpless person who ever lived, God is willing to take you—if you will submit to Him—and work through you in the most marvelous manner by His mighty word. He loves to do it. He has "chosen the weak things of the world to confound the things that are mighty; and the base things of the world, and things which are despised, hath God chosen, yea, and things which are not, to bring to naught things that are: that no flesh should glory in His presence." 1 Cor. 1:27-29.

He says, "Whosoever heareth these sayings of Mine, and doeth them, I will liken him unto a wise man, which built his house upon a rock." Then, by receiving God's word into your heart and allowing the word to work, you are building on immovable rock. But Jesus Himself is in the word, and is the

17

Word (see John 1 and 6), so humbly receiving the Word brings Jesus into your heart to work. And so your work is to submit and receive, and Jesus the living Word supplies all the power and does all the work through you, if you will let Him.

It is not enough for you to unite yourself to someone else who is united to Christ. You must for yourself come to Christ the Word as to a living stone, and build on Him. Then you become a living stone, because you partake of the life of the living Foundation. You grow on the Foundation until you are a part of the Foundation, and the Foundation is a part of you. Is it any wonder, then, that you have strength, and that you can stand unmoved through all the storms and tempests of life?

Then when you look at the grass and realize your frailty, and your helplessness, don't become discouraged, but rather lift your eyes in thankfulness to heaven and praise that mighty One who can take you—the weakest and most helpless of His creatures—and by His word strengthen you "with all might according to His glorious power."

~6~

Overcoming in Christ

To His disciples Jesus said, "In the world ye shall have tribulation; but be of good cheer; I have overcome the world." John 16:33.

Why should this fact cause you to be of good cheer? Why should you rejoice because someone else has overcome the world when you must overcome it also? The grand truth which answers this question is that you are not an overcomer in yourself, but an overcomer in Christ.

To the Corinthians the apostle writes, "Now thanks be unto God, which always causeth us to triumph in Christ, and maketh manifest the savour of His knowledge by us in every place." 2 Cor. 2:14. How is it that you are always caused to triumph in Christ? It is simply because Christ has triumphed over everything, and in Him victory is yours.

Christ was tempted in all points like as we are, yet was without sin. He has met and overcome every obstacle that can possibly be brought against your humanity in the struggle with temptation. And whenever "the world, the flesh, and the devil" meet Him, they meet their Conqueror. The victory has already been won. And therefore in Christ you have the victory; for when you are in Him, the temptations assail Him, and not you by yourself. When you hide your weakness in His strength then His strength will fight the battle. He has gained the victory, and the beaten foe can never recover from his defeat so as to hope for victory over Him.

What, then, must you do to overcome? And why is it that you are so often overcome? The obvious answer is that you cannot overcome outside of Christ. What you have to do is to take the victory that has already been won, the victory that He gained. He overcame for you so that He might bestow His triumph on you. And you take His victory by faith, for it is by faith that Christ comes into your heart.

This is what is meant by the apostle John, when he says, "This is the victory that overcometh the world, even our faith." 1 John 5:4. By faith you bring Christ into your heart and life. Eph. 3:17. He is there as the Conqueror of all that is to be met and overcome in the Christian warfare.

The glorious truth is revealed that the victory over every temptation and difficulty is already yours, in Christ. Therefore you don't need to come to the conflict with a faint heart, but with all confidence, knowing that defeat cannot possibly be the outcome, no matter how formidable the foe may make himself appear. The battle is already fought, and Jesus Christ holds out to you the victory. You have to simply take it, and say, "Thanks be to God, which giveth us the victory through our Lord Jesus Christ." 1 Cor. 15:57.

~7~

The Indwelling Word

"Let the word of Christ dwell in you richly in all wisdom." Col. 3:16. Rightly understood, this text solves the problem of Christian living. So let's spend a few minutes to see how much is involved in it.

It can't be doubted that there is power in the word of God, far above that of any other book. The Lord through the prophet Jeremiah rebukes the false prophets, who speak their own words instead of the words of God, and says: "What is the chaff to the wheat?" "Is not My word like as a fire? Saith the LORD; and like a hammer that breaketh the rock in pieces?" Jer. 23:28, 29.

The word hidden in your heart protects against sin. "Thy word have I hid in mine heart, that I might not sin against Thee." Ps. 119:11. And of the righteous we read that the reason why none of his steps slide, is that "the law of his God is in his heart." Ps. 37:31. David also says: "By the word of Thy lips I have kept me from the paths of the destroyer." Ps. 17:4.

The word of the Lord is the seed by which you are born again. The Apostle Peter says: "Seeing ye have purified your souls in obeying the truth through the Spirit unto unfeigned love of the brethren, see that ye love one another with a pure heart fervently; being born again, not of corruptible seed, but of incorruptible, by the word of God, which liveth and abideth forever." 1 Peter 1:22, 23. When you become Christ's you are born again by the Spirit, and the word of God is the seed from which you are developed into a new creature in Christ.

The word has power to give life. It is itself "quick," that is, alive, and powerful; and the Psalmist prays to be quickened, made alive, according to the word, and then says: "This is my comfort in my affliction; for Thy word hath quickened me." Ps. 119:25, 50.

Jesus states this plainly in John 6:63: "It is the Spirit that quickeneth; the flesh profiteth nothing; the words that I speak unto you, they are spirit, and they are life." This shows that the power of the Spirit of God dwells in the word of God.

With the knowledge that the word of God is the seed by which you are born unto a new life, and that hiding the word in your heart keeps you from sin, you may easily understand 1 John 3:9: "Whosoever is born of God doth not commit sin; for His seed remaineth in him; and he cannot sin, because he is born of God." How simple! There is in the word that divine energy which can transform your mind, and make you a new creation "which after God is created in righteousness and true holiness." Of course the word can do this only if you receive it in simple faith. But the word does not lose any of its power. If your soul thus born again retains that sacred, powerful word by which you were born, it will keep you still a new creature. It is as powerful to preserve as it is to create.

Jesus, our great example, gave us an illustration of this. When tempted on every point by the devil, his only reply was, "It is written," followed by a text of Scripture that met the temptation exactly. If you would stand fast you must do the same thing. There is no other way. Here is an illustration in David's words, "By the word of Thy lips I have kept me from the paths of the destroyer."

In speaking of the casting down of the "accuser of our brethren," the heavenly voice says: "And they overcame him by the blood of the Lamb, and by the word of their testimony." Rev. 12:11. The word of their testimony is the word of God that the Psalmist delighted in. They overcame Satan by the blood of the Lamb, and by the word of God.

This can only be done when you have the word of God abiding in you. The Spirit is given to bring truth to your memory in time of trial; but if you haven't learned it then you won't be able to remember it. But if you have hidden the word in your heart, the Spirit will remind you of it when you are tempted. He will bring to your memory just the word that will foil the tempter.

Every Christian can testify as to the power of the word at such times. When inclined to congratulate yourself on some real or fancied superior attainment, what a powerful check are the words, "Who maketh thee to differ from another? And what hast thou that thou didst not receive? Now if thou didst receive it, why dost thou glory, as if thou hadst not received it?" 1 Cor. 4:7. Or when harsh and bitter thoughts are struggling within you for control, what power to quell those turbulent emotions lies in the words, "Charity suffereth long, and is kind; charity envieth not; charity vaunteth not itself, is not puffed up, doth not behave itself unseemly, seeketh not her own, is not easily provoked, thinketh no evil." 1 Cor. 13:4, 5. When provoked almost beyond endurance, how the gentle rebuke, "The servant of the Lord must not strive; but be gentle unto all men," helps you to be calm. Add to this the many "exceeding great and precious promises" which bring victory to your soul as you grasp them by faith. Thousands of aged Christians can testify to the miraculous power resting in a few simple words of the Scriptures.

Where does the power come from? The answer is found in the words of Christ: "The words which I speak unto you, they are spirit and they are life." What spirit are they? The Spirit of Christ. So the power of the Spirit dwells in the word. Truly, Christ himself dwells in the word, for He is the Word.

Can you understand the mystery of inspiration? Only if you can understand the mystery of the incarnation; for both are the same. "The Word was made flesh." We cannot understand how Christ could be all the fullness of the Godhead, and at the same time be in the form of a servant, subject to all the infirmities of mortal flesh. Neither can we understand how the Bible could be written by fallible mortals, exhibiting the peculiarities of each, and yet be the pure, unadulterated word of God. But it is certainly true that the power that was in the Word that was made flesh, is the power that is in the word that the apostles and prophets have written for us.

Now you can begin to appreciate the power residing in the word. "By the word of the LORD were the heavens made; and all the host of them by the breath of His mouth." Ps. 33:6. Christ, by whom the worlds were made, upholds them "by the word of His power." Heb. 1:3. The power that resides in the words of revelation, is the power that could speak the worlds into existence, and can keep them in their appointed places. Surely it is worth your while to take time to study and meditate on the word.

In doing this you bring Christ Himself into your heart. In John 15, the Lord exhorts you to abide in Him, and to allow Him to abide in you; and then a few verses later He speaks of you abiding in Him, and His word abiding in you. John 15:4, 7. It is by His word that Christ abides in your heart; for Paul says that Christ will dwell in your heart by faith (Eph. 3:17); and "faith cometh by hearing, and hearing by the word of God." Rom. 10:17.

Many people earnestly long for Christ to come and dwell in their hearts, and they imagine that the reason why He does not do so is because they are not good enough, and they vainly set about trying to get so good that He can condescend to come in. They forget that Christ comes into your heart, not because it is free from sin, but in order to free it from sin; and possibly they never realized that Christ is in the word, and that if you will make it a constant companion, and will yield yourself to its influence, you will have Christ dwelling within. When you have hidden the word in your heart, you meditate on it day and night, and you believe it with the simple faith of a child—then you have Christ dwelling in your heart by faith, and you will experience His mighty, creative power.

Isn't this thought encouraging? When you come to God in secret prayer, and the Spirit brings to your remembrance some precious promise or needed reproof, isn't it encouraging to know that as you accept them, Christ is coming into your heart with the same power that created the worlds from nothing? Doesn't it clothe the word with new dignity? No wonder David could never tire of sounding its praises. May the thought that God is in the word be a fresh incentive to you to gain strength for your work by taking more time to feed on the source of divine strength.

~8~

Faith and Breath

"The just shall live by faith." Rom. 1:17. That means that your whole life will be faith, as the Apostle Paul said, "The life which I now live in the flesh I live by the faith of the Son of God, who loved me, and gave Himself for me." Gal. 2:20. Faith is not a thing of a moment; if you believe a thing today, and are in doubt about it tomorrow, you don't have faith. Faith is continuous; it is an everlasting foundation. You live by breathing. You cannot live by breathing one day, and ceasing to breathe the next day. As soon as you cease to breathe, you cease to live. So it is with faith; when your faith ceases, your righteous life ceases. If you exercise faith as often and as long as you breathe, you will be righteous as long as you live.

~9~

Present Salvation

God inhabits eternity, so that all time is present with Him, so all His promises and blessings for you are in the present tense. This makes Him "a very present help in trouble," for you can only live in the present. You cannot live one moment in the future. You expect things in the future, and have hope of things to come, but the present is all that you can ever have, for when the things come that you hope for, they will be present. The things which you have reason to hope for in the future, will be the continuation of the things which you have now. All things are in Christ, and His promise is, "Lo, I am with you always, even unto the end of the world." Matt. 28:20.

The apostle Paul blessed God because He "hath blessed us with all spiritual blessings in heavenly things in Christ Jesus." Eph. 1:3. The promises of God for the future must be present realities to you, if you ever receive any benefit from them. "For all the promises of God in Him are yea, and in Him Amen, unto the glory of God by us." 2 Cor. 1:20. It is by these "exceeding great and precious promises" that you are made "partakers of the Divine nature." The glories of the world to come will be but the revealing of that which you have now in the personal presence within you of the Lord Jesus Christ. The only hope of glory is Christ in you.

"Jesus Christ is the same yesterday, and today, and forever." Heb. 13:8. The word of God "liveth and abideth forever." 1 Peter 1:23. You do not have to deal with a dead word, which was spoken so long ago that there is no more force in it, but with a word which has the same life as though it were just spoken.

Indeed it is of benefit to you only when you receive it as spoken directly and personally to you. "When ye received the word of God which ye heard of us, ye received it not as the word of men, but as it is in truth the word of God, which effectually worketh also in you that believe." 1 Thess. 2:13. "All Scripture is given by inspiration of God, and is profitable." 2 Tim. 3:16. It is all in the present.

For this reason you can never outgrow the Scriptures. There is not a single text in the Bible that has become obsolete. There is none that the Christian of the longest experience has outgrown, so that he has no need of it. There is none that can be laid aside. The text which brings you to the Savior, is the text which is ever needed to keep you there. And although your mind has expanded, and your spiritual sight has been greatly strengthened the word still has meaning because every word of God is of infinite depth. So as your mind expands, the word means more to you than it did in the beginning.

The universe appears much greater to the astronomer than it does to someone who has never looked through a telescope. You look at the stars with your eyes and they seem very far off. Then you look at them through a powerful telescope and although you can see so much farther with it, the distance to the stars seems to be very much greater than it did with your limited vision. So the more you become acquainted with the word of God, the greater it becomes. The promises of God, which seemed so exceedingly great when they first appeared to you, become much more exceedingly great the more you consider them and apply them.

The word of God is a light shining in a dark place. 2 Peter 1:19. It is the revelation of Christ, who is the Light of the world, therefore it is a lamp. Ps. 119:105; Prov. 6:23. We have heard of the young sailor who was left in charge of the helm, with instructions to hold the ship's head straight toward a certain star, which was pointed out to him, and who, in a few hours, called the captain and said that he wanted another star to steer by, as he had sailed past the first one given him. What was the trouble? He had turned the ship round, and was sailing away from the star. So it is with those who say that they have outgrown certain portions of the Bible. The trouble is that they have turned their backs on it.

What is the Gospel? "It is the power of God unto salvation to

27

everyone that believeth." Rom. 1:16. It is present power applied to your salvation when you have present faith. From what does the power of God save you? Jesus is the power of God and it was said of Him, "Thou shalt call His name Jesus; for He shall save His people from their sins." Matt. 1:21. "This is a faithful saying, and worthy of all acceptation, that Christ Jesus came into the world to save sinners." 1 Tim. 1:15. The Gospel is the power of God to save you from sin. But it is present power, for sin is ever present. Its power is applied only while you are believing. "The just shall live by faith." Rom. 1:17. The moment you cease to believe, then you are a sinner, just the same as if you had never believed. Yesterday's faith will not answer for today, any more than your breathing yesterday will keep you alive today.

The message of the Lord to you immediately before His coming is, "Thou sayest I am rich and increased with goods, and have need of nothing; and knowest not that thou art wretched, and miserable, and poor, and blind and naked." Rev. 3:17. Have you outgrown this text? No. The blessing comes to you as you acknowledge the truth of the Lord's charge; then the Lord will come to you to supply all your needs. It is when you say, "Lord, be merciful to me, a sinner," that you go down to your house justified.

And it is only as you continue to utter that prayer, that you are justified. "For every one that exalteth himself shall be abased; and he that humbleth himself shall be exalted." Luke 18:14. The apostle says: "This is a faithful saying, and worthy of all acceptation, that Christ Jesus came into the world to save sinners; of whom I am chief." 1 Tim. 1:15. Note that he does not say, "Of whom I was chief;" but "of whom I am chief." And it was when he acknowledged himself to be the chief of sinners, that the mercy and longsuffering of God was exhibited in him as the chief.

Some wonder whether a Christian ought to sing these lines in Wesley's blessed hymn:

> "Just and holy is Thy name,
> I am all unrighteousness;
> Vile and full of sin I am;
> Thou art full of truth and grace."

If you think that you have outgrown those lines you are in a pitiable condition, for you are shutting yourself off from the source of righteousness. "There is none good, but One; that is, God." Matt. 19:17. Therefore, whatever righteousness is ever exhibited in you must only be the righteousness of God. It is only when you acknowledge your own sinfulness, that you will lay hold on the righteousness of God that is by the faith of Christ. It is only by the obedience of One that you are made righteous. Rom. 5:19. And that One is Christ.

"And He is the propitiation for our sins; and not for ours only, but also for the sins of the whole world." 1 John 2:2. The Christian of forty years' experience is just as much in need of the righteousness which comes through Christ, as is the sinner who is now for the first time coming to the Lord. So we read, "If we walk in the light, as He is in the light, we have fellowship one with another, and the blood of Jesus Christ His Son cleanseth us from all sin. If we say that we have no sin, we deceive ourselves and the truth is not in us." 1 John 1:7, 8. The most that you can say is that Christ is without sin, and that Christ has given Himself for you. He is of God "made unto us wisdom, and righteousness, and sanctification, and redemption." 1 Cor. 1:30. But note that cleansing is a present process. You may know that the blood of Christ cleansed you from sin at some time in the past; but that will do you no good. His life is continually needed, in order that the cleansing may go on continually. You are "saved by His life." Rom. 5:10. For Christ is your life. Col. 3:4.

So it is that "every spirit that confesseth that Jesus Christ is come in the flesh is of God; and every spirit that confesseth not that Jesus Christ is come in the flesh is not of God." 1 John 4:2, 3. Note again the present tense. It is not enough to confess that Jesus Christ did come in the flesh; that will not bring you salvation. You must confess from positive knowledge, that Jesus is just now come in the flesh, and then you are of God. Christ came in the flesh two thousand years ago, just to demonstrate this. He did it once and He is able to do it again. If you deny the possibility of His coming in your flesh now, then you deny the possibility of His ever having come in the flesh.

So your part is to confess with humility of mind that you are a sinner; that you have no good thing in you. If you do not do this, then the truth is not in you; but if you do, then Christ, who came into the world for the express purpose of saving sinners, will come and take up His abode with you, and then the truth will surely be in you. Then perfection will be manifested in the midst of imperfection. You will have completeness in the midst of weakness. For we "are complete in Him." Col. 2:10. He has created all things by the word of His power and so He can take you who are but nothing, and can make you "to the praise of the glory of His grace." Eph. 1:6. "For of Him, and through Him, and to Him are all things; to whom be the glory for ever. Amen." Rom. 11:36.

~10~

The Christian Life

It was said: "The child at school looks at the copy in the writing book, and imitates it, trying to write each line better. That is the Christian life, and that is all of it."

Is that all of it? Not by any means. If it were all of it, there would be no hope for you; for the pattern is Jesus Christ, in whom dwelleth "all the fullness of the Godhead bodily," and you can never, ever, successfully copy His life. "For my thoughts are not your thoughts, neither are your ways My ways, saith the LORD. For as the heavens are higher than the earth, so are My ways higher than your ways, and My thoughts than your thoughts." Isa. 55:8, 9. If you would copy the life of Christ as the schoolboy copies his lesson, and do it successfully, you must have power equal to that of God.

If the boy whose hand the master holds and guides in imitating the copy, were used as an illustration of the Christian life, it would be a step nearer the truth; but even that would not be the truth. That is mechanical. The boy may yield his hand willingly to the master, that it may be guided, but the writing is after all not his own. God does not use you as a dead instrument to be operated on, although you are to yield yourself as an instrument of righteousness to Him.

The Christian life is simply the life of Christ. If the master who sets the copy for the schoolboy, could put all his own skill and power into that boy, so that what he writes will not be merely an imitation of the master's copy, but the master's own writing, and still the free act of the boy, we should have an excellent illustration of the Christian life. "Work out your own salvation with fear and trembling. For it is God which worketh in you both to will and to do of His good pleasure." Phil. 2:12, 13. "I live; yet not I, but Christ liveth in me; and the life that I now live in the flesh I live by the faith of the Son of God, who loved me, and gave Himself for me." Gal. 2:20.

"He that saith he abideth in Him ought himself also so to walk even as He walked." 1 John 2:6. And how was it that He walked? Christ Himself said, "The Father that dwelleth in Me, He doeth the works." John 14:10. Christ has set you the copy, but instead of standing off and watching you try to imitate Him, He gladly comes in to your heart, becoming one with you, so that His life is your life, and His acts are yours. This is life—your Christian life.

~11~

Desperately Wicked

Quite likely you would be offended and shocked if one of your friends told you that you were a desperately wicked person, or if someone would describe you that way publicly. You know some people who are wicked—perhaps some of them you consider to be desperately wicked. And you have read of such people in history and in the accounts of crime which fill the news stories; and you would not wish to be classed with them. You belong to the "respectable" class of people—that class who are not as good as they might be, but who do not do anything very bad. It would certainly be a gross libel to point you out as desperately wicked.

Would it? Let's consider this matter a little. The Lord has said something on the point, and He does not libel people, but tells everyone the exact truth. Jeremiah says, "The heart is deceitful above all things, and desperately wicked." Jer. 17:9. Whose heart is it? Ah, there are no particular people specified in the statement; its application is general; it means your heart and mine. Neither does it say your heart may become deceitful and desperately wicked, but it is that way already. There is no getting around it; the Lord says your heart is deceitful above all things, and desperately wicked. No matter about your respectability and standing in society; if the human heart rules within you then you are desperately wicked. And it is only because your heart is so deceitful that you do not realize the fact. Yes; there is murder there; there is adultery, there is theft and blasphemy, there is that dreadful crime which shocked you when you read it, and for which a man was executed; there is everything of which lawless people are guilty, and which is contrary to the Ten Commandments. The Lord says so; for He says, "The carnal mind is enmity against God; for it is not subject to the law of God, neither indeed can be." Rom. 8:7.

To how much of the law of God is the carnal mind not subject? Can it be subject to part of the law, and not subject to the remaining part? Certainly that cannot be. Your heart must either be subject to the law in its entirety, or not subject to it at all; and the carnal heart, as the text declares, "is not subject to the law of God." This carnal nature is the nature you get by birth, and this nature you must retain, no matter what your station and occupation is, until you allow the Lord to transform your heart by the power of His grace. And therefore when this natural, or carnal heart, exists, you are at enmity with every law in the Ten Commandments. You are not only at enmity with the command which says, "Thou shalt not covet,"—as very respectable people can be—but you are also not in harmony with the commands which say, "Thou shalt not kill," and "Thou shalt not commit adultery." You may not feel the enmity stirring you up to commit some shocking deed; but nevertheless, it is there.

Even if you think you are a good person, do you know what is in your heart? How often do circumstances reveal evils that you didn't dream of? Let your nature become suddenly ruffled, and words and deeds spring forth which cause you surprise and shame. People don't start out in life to become murderers or adulterers or burglars. Such ones would be horrified if you told them at the beginning what the developments of later years would bring. Their nature was the same as yours; the evil deeds were there.

There is no use denying what the Lord tells you. If mere "respectability" could decide the question the devil would have the advantage over you, for he is "transformed into an angel of light" (2 Cor. 11:14), and you don't have that power. You can't compete with the devil in good appearance. The Lord sees you just as you are, and the sooner you see yourself as He sees you, the better. When you become convinced that you really are desperately wicked, you will see the necessity of getting rid of your inherited carnal heart altogether, instead of trying to make it presentable to God by your efforts at patching it up. You will be ready to accept the new heart which God gives you on condition of perfect submission to Him. You will be willing to receive Jesus Christ who dwells in your heart by faith. It is for you to choose between a heart that is desperately wicked and one that is infinitely good.

~12~

Hear and Live

Eight of the Ten Commandments begin with the words "Thou shalt not." They are not merely negative, however, for they are all summed up in the two great positive commandments, "Thou shalt love the Lord thy God with all thy heart, and with all thy soul, and with all thy mind," and, "Thou shalt love thy neighbor as thyself."

Too often these are regarded as mere arbitrary commands, but they are much more than that. There is a power in them that does not pertain to ordinary words. It is the power of the word of God, which is life itself. Christ said, "The words that I speak unto you, they are spirit, and they are life." John 6:63. Being the very Spirit of life, they give life to all who hear them.

The life giving power of the word of the Lord is demonstrated in the resurrection of Lazarus and the ruler's daughter. Christ said: "Verily, verily, I say unto you, The hour is coming, and now is, when the dead shall hear the voice of the Son of God; and they that hear shall live." John 5:25. Then follows the statement that as the Father has life in Himself, so has He given to the Son to have life in Himself, so that when the hour comes all that are in their graves shall hear His voice, and shall come forth.

"Faith cometh by hearing, and hearing by the word of God." Rom. 10:17. "With the heart man believeth." The hearing of faith puts the words of God in your heart. But Christ dwells in your heart by faith (Eph. 3:17), because His Spirit is in His word; so that the hearing of faith brings the life of Christ into your heart, and that is righteousness.

But this puts the law in your heart; for when Moses admonished the people to keep the commandments he said, "For this commandment which I command thee this day, it is not hidden from thee, neither is it far off. It is not in heaven, that thou shouldest say, Who shall go up for us to heaven, and bring it unto us, that we may hear it, and do it? Neither is it beyond the sea, that thou shouldest say, Who shall go over the sea for us, and bring it unto us, that we may hear it, and do it? But the word is very nigh unto thee, in thy mouth, and in thy heart, that thou mayest do it." Deut. 30:11-14.

In Romans 10, just before the apostle's conclusion that faith comes by hearing, and hearing by the word of God, this passage from Deuteronomy is quoted, and it is shown that the "commandment" refers to Christ, who is the soul and substance of the law. And that this is what Moses meant by the words is shown from Paul's statement that the words of Moses are the language of "the righteousness which is of faith." And further, by the words of Moses himself: "I call heaven and earth to record this day against you, that I have set before you life and death, blessing and cursing; therefore choose life, that both thou and thy seed may live; that thou mayest love the LORD thy God, and that thou mayest obey His voice, and that thou mayest cleave unto Him; for He is thy life, and the length of thy days." Deut. 30:19, 20.

Life comes through keeping the commandments (Matt. 19:17; Rev. 22:14); but Christ is the life of the law, and He dwells in your heart by faith in His word. Thus the law as the real righteousness of God, and not the mere form, is life, and has power to give life. David said, "This is my comfort in my affliction; for Thy word hath quickened me." Ps. 119:50.

"Hear, O Israel; the LORD our God is one LORD; and thou shalt love the LORD thy God with all thine heart, and with all thy soul, and with all thy might. And these words, which I command thee this day, shall be in thine heart." Deut. 6:4-6. How are they in your heart? By faith. And how does faith come? By hearing. The idea is that, just as at the last day those who hear the voice of God will be raised to life, out of their graves, so now those who really hear His commandments will receive life from them. Accordingly the Lord testified as follows: "Hear, O My people and I will testify unto thee; O Israel, if thou wilt hearken unto

Me, there shall no strange god be in thee; neither shalt thou worship any strange god." Ps. 81:8, 9.

If the children of Israel had only listened to the Lord continually, He would have assured their salvation. While they were listening to Him, He would have taken on Himself the responsibility of keeping them free from idolatry and all sin. So when in the law, He says "Thou shalt not," He does not simply mean to forbid you from doing the things spoken of, but also to assure you that you will not do them if you but hear in faith, recognizing Him in them.

One thing should not be lost sight of, and that is that the righteousness which comes by the hearing of faith is not a mere passive righteousness. It is the active righteousness of God. And, moreover, it is just that righteousness which is demanded in the Ten Commandments, without any variation. If you hear God you must hear the very words of God, and the Ten Commandments are the words that God spoke with His own voice. He did not say, "The first day is the Sabbath of the Lord," but He did say, "The seventh day is the Sabbath of the LORD thy God." Since God never commanded the observance of the first day of the week, you can't hear those words from His mouth; consequently you can't receive life or righteousness by observing Sunday.

"Man shall not live by bread alone, but by every word that proceedeth out of the mouth of God;" "He that hath an ear to hear, let him hear." But "take heed how ye hear."

~13~

The Power of Forgiveness

"And, behold, they brought to him a man sick of the palsy, lying on a bed; and Jesus seeing their faith said unto the sick of the palsy; Son, be of good cheer; thy sins be forgiven thee. And, behold, certain of the scribes said within themselves, This man blasphemeth. And Jesus knowing their thoughts said, Wherefore think ye evil in your hearts? For whether is easier, to say, Thy sins be forgiven thee; or to say, Arise, and walk? But that ye may know that the Son of man hath power on earth to forgive sins, then saith He to the sick of the palsy, Arise, take up thy bed, and go unto thine house. And he arose, and departed to his house. But when the multitudes saw it, they marveled, and glorified God, which had given such power unto men." Matt. 9:2-8.

Christians often say, "I can understand and believe that God will forgive my sins, but it is hard for me to believe that He can keep me from sinning." These have much to learn about what is meant by forgiveness of sins. It is true that they often have a measure of peace in believing that God does forgive their sins. But they deprive themselves of much blessing through their failure to grasp the power of forgiveness.

"These are written, that ye might believe that Jesus is the Christ, the Son of God; and that believing ye might have life through His name." The scribes did not believe that Jesus could forgive sin. In order to show that He had power to forgive sins, He healed the paralyzed man. This miracle was worked for the express purpose of illustrating the work of forgiving sin, and demonstrating its power. Jesus said to the paralyzed man, "Arise, take up thy bed, and go unto thine house," that you might know

His power to forgive sin. So the power exhibited in the healing of that man is the power given to you in the forgiveness of your sins.

Note particularly that the effect of the words of Jesus continued after they were spoken. They made a change in the man, and that change was permanent. It works the same way in the forgiveness of sin. It's easy to think that when God forgives your sins that the change is in God and not in you, that God finally ceases to hold anything against you. But this implies that God had a grievance against you, which is not the case. God is not a man; He does not hold a grudge against you. It is not because He has a hard feeling in his heart against you that He forgives you, but because of something in your heart. God is all right; you are all wrong. So God forgives you so that you may also be all right.

To illustrate the forgiveness of sin, Jesus said to the man, "Arise, take up thy bed, and go unto thine house." The man arose, obedient to His voice. The power that was in the words of Jesus, raised him up, and made him well.

The power that removed his paralysis and gave him strength remained in him as long as he kept the faith. This is illustrated by the Psalmist, when he says: "I waited patiently for the LORD; and He inclined unto me, and heard my cry. He brought me up also out of an horrible pit, out of the miry clay, and set my feet upon a rock, and established my goings." Ps. 40:1, 2.

There is life in the words of God. Jesus said, "The words that I speak unto you, they are spirit, and they are life." John 6:63. The word received in faith brings the Spirit and the life of God to your soul. So when you hear the words, "Son, be of good cheer, thy sins be forgiven thee," and receive those words in penitence, as the living words of the living God, a new life is begun in you and you are a different person. It is the power of God's forgiveness, and that alone, that keeps you from sinning. If you continue to sin after you receive pardon, it is because you have not grasped the fullness of the blessing that was given to you in the forgiveness of your sins.

In the story we read the man received new life. His paralyzed condition was his natural life wasting away. He was partially dead. The words of Christ gave him fresh life. This new life that was given to his body enabled him to walk. This is an illustration to you of the unseen life of God which he had received in the words, "Thy sins be forgiven thee," and which made him a new creature in Christ.

This simple and clear illustration will help you understand some of the words of the apostle Paul. "Giving thanks unto the Father, which hath made us meet to be partakers of the inheritance of the saints in light; who hath delivered us from the power of darkness, and hath translated us into the kingdom of His dear Son; in whom we have redemption through his blood, even the forgiveness of sins." Col 1:12-14. See the same statement concerning redemption through Christ's blood, in 1 Peter 1:18, 19; Rev. 5:9.

Notice two points: You have redemption through Christ's blood, and this redemption is the forgiveness of sins. But the blood is the life. See Gen. 9:4; Rev. 17:13, 14. Therefore Col. 1:14 is telling you that you have redemption through Christ's life. But doesn't the Scripture say that we are reconciled to God by the death of His Son? It does, and that is just what is taught here. Christ "gave Himself for us, that He might redeem us from all iniquity." Titus 2:14. He "gave Himself for our sins." Gal. 1:4. In giving Himself, He gives His life. In shedding His blood, He pours out His life. But in giving up His life, He gives it to you. His life is righteousness, even the perfect righteousness of God, so that when you receive it you are "made the righteousness of God in Him." It is the receiving of Christ's life, as you are baptized into His death, that reconciles you to God. That is how you "put on the new man which after God is created in righteousness and true holiness," "after the image of Him that created him." Eph. 4:24; Col. 3:10.

Now read Rom. 3:23-25, and it will be easier to understand: "For all have sinned, and come short of the glory of God; being justified [that is, made righteous, or doers of the law] freely by His grace through the redemption that is in Christ Jesus; whom God hath set forth to be a propitiation through faith in His blood, to declare His righteousness for the remission [sending away] of sins that are past, through the forbearance of God."

You have sinned. Your whole life has been sin. Even your thoughts have been evil. Mark 7:21. And to be carnally minded is death. Therefore your life of sin is a living death. If you are not set free, you will die an eternal death. You have no ability to get righteousness out of the holy law of God, so God in His mercy puts His own righteousness on you when you believe. As a free gift, out of the riches of His grace, He makes you righteous. He does this by His words. He declares—speaks—His righteousness unto and on you through your faith in the blood of Christ. In Him is God's righteousness, "for in Him dwelleth all the fullness of the Godhead bodily."

When He speaks the righteousness of God on you this takes away your sin. God takes away your sinful life by putting His own righteous life in its place. This is the power of the forgiveness of sin. It is "the power of an endless life."

When you receive the life of God by faith your Christian life begins. How do you continue? The same way you began. "As ye have therefore received Christ Jesus the Lord, so walk ye in Him." Col. 2:6. For "the just shall live by faith." The secret of living the Christian life is simply to hold fast to the life of Christ, which you received from Him when He forgave your sins. God forgives your sin by taking it away. He justified you by making you godly. He reconciles your rebellious self to Himself by taking away your rebellion and making you loyal and obedient.

Is it difficult for you to understand how you can have the life of God as an actual fact? Does it seem unreal because you have it by faith? It was by faith that the poor paralyzed man received new life and strength. Was his strength any less real? Wasn't it an actual fact that he received strength? You can't understand it? Of course not, for it is a manifestation of "the love of God that passeth knowledge." But you may believe it, and realize the fact, and then you will have eternity to study the wonder of it. Read again and again the story of the healing of the paralyzed man, and meditate on it until it is a living reality to you. Then remember that "these are written that ye might believe that Jesus is the Christ, the Son of God, and that believing ye might have life through His name."

~14~

Eve Disbelieved God

If Eve had believed the word of God she never would have sinned.

Yea, so long as Eve had believed the word of God, she never could have sinned. If you will think about this you will agree that it is true.

She had the word of God plainly expressed: "Of the tree of the knowledge of good and evil, thou shalt not eat of it: for in the day that thou eatest thereof thou shalt surely die."

Satan came with his new word, his arguments and persuasions: "Ye shall not surely die; for God doth know that in the day ye eat thereof, then your eyes shall be opened, and ye shall be like God, knowing good and evil."

If Eve had said: "No; God said that I must not eat of that tree. He said that in the day I eat of it I will die. I believe God. I do not claim to understand it, but He does understand it. I will trust Him. I will not eat of that tree." If she had done this she never would have sinned. And as long as she had continued to believe, she could not have sinned.

So it is eternally true that if Eve had believed God, she never would have sinned. And as long as she believed God, she never could have sinned. And the same with Adam.

Now this is just as true today as it was that day; and it is just as true of you today as it was of Eve that day.

Today, if you believe God, you will not sin; and as long as you believe God, you cannot sin. This principle is eternal, and it is as good today as it was in the beginning. And Christ in our human nature has demonstrated it.

But this requires really believing God. Not a pretended believing, that apparently accepts one word of the Lord and rejects another; that professes to believe one statement of the word of God, and doubts the next one. That way of doing is not believing God at all.

This also calls for readiness and diligence, a hungering and thirsting, to know the word of God, that will lead you on and on to know all that the Lord has spoken. Of course if you would rather sin than search to know and believe the word of God, that you may not sin, there is no power in the universe that can keep you from sinning. But if you abhor sin, and you would rather die than sin—to you the word of God is precious; to you it is a pleasure, yes, a joy, to study to find all the Lord has spoken. With you there is a hungering and thirsting that will gladly receive the word of God, that you may not sin.

"Concerning the works of men, by the word of Thy lips I have kept me from the paths of the destroyer." Ps. 17:4.

"Thy words were found, and I did eat them; and Thy word was unto me the joy and rejoicing of mine heart." Jer. 15:16.

"Study to show thyself approved unto God." 2 Tim. 2:15.

"Let the word of Christ dwell in you richly." Col 3:16.

"Thy word have I hid in mine heart, that I might not sin against Thee." Ps 119:11.

And so you will certainly be "kept by the power of God through faith unto salvation ready" *now* "to be revealed," because it is the last time. 1 Peter 1:5.

~15~

Another Man

There is something exceedingly comforting in the thought of receiving the power of the Holy Spirit; and no wonder, for the Spirit is the Comforter. But the great comfort of it is shown in the result, as illustrated in one typical case. When Samuel had anointed Saul king over Israel, he said to him:

"Thou shalt meet a company of prophets coming down from the high place with a psaltery, and a tabret, and a pipe, and a harp, before them; and they shall prophesy; and the Spirit of the LORD will come upon thee, and thou shalt prophesy with them, and shalt be turned into another man." 1 Sam. 10:5, 6.

What a wonderfully pleasant thought, that the Spirit turns the one who yields to its presence into another man. The old man is sinful. We are carnal by nature. We have done many wicked deeds, because sin is our very nature. The memories of those sins have often appalled us, as the knowledge of the sinful nature, from which they came, has often been to us a grief and shame. Past misdeeds which we could not wipe out, have been held up before us by Satan to discourage us, and thus to give him greater power over our sinful nature.

But now the glorious news comes to us that by yielding to the Spirit of God, we may be turned into other people. That "new man" is "created in righteousness and true holiness." Eph. 4:24. It takes the place of "the old man, which is corrupt according to the deceitful lusts." This new man is "renewed in knowledge after the image of Him that created him" (Col. 3:10); and this renewing takes place "day by day." 2 Cor. 4:16.

45

We yield, and the transformation takes place. We continue to yield, and renewing continually takes place. And now the devil comes to us again with his old tricks. He presents the long list of sins, but they do not appall us anymore. We can say to him, "You have made a mistake; the man who used to live here, and who committed those sins, is dead, and I have no connection with him, and therefore cannot be called on to settle his accounts." There is no more a "fearful looking for of judgment," for we shall not come into judgment, having passed from death unto life. John 5:24.

The devil tries his old temptations, through the lusts of the flesh, but again he is baffled. He used to have no difficulty in leading us astray, but now he has another man to deal with, and to his astonishment he finds that his purposes fail. We are not condemned, because we walk in the Spirit.

This new man has never sinned, because it is "created in righteousness and true holiness," and kept eternally new. How often we have wished that we might get rid of ourselves. We may. The word comes to us, "Put off the old man, with his deeds," and with the word comes the power to put him off. And the new man cannot sin, because it is the very image of God. So that our part day by day may be to declare from the heart with the Apostle Paul:

"For I through the law am dead to the law, that I might live unto God. I am crucified with Christ; nevertheless I live; yet not I, but Christ liveth in me; and the life which I now live in the flesh I live by the faith of the Son of God, who loved me, and gave Himself for me." Gal. 2:19, 20.

~16~

As Free as a Bird

Jesus Christ began His earthly ministry by reading in the synagogue at Nazareth the following words from Isaiah: "The Spirit of the Lord is upon Me, because He hath anointed Me to preach the Gospel to the poor; He hath sent Me to heal the brokenhearted, to preach deliverance to the captives, and recovering of sight to the blind, to set at liberty them that are bruised, to proclaim the acceptable year of the Lord." Luke 4:18, 19. And then He said to the congregation, "This day is this scripture fulfilled in your ears."

Turning to the place that Christ read from, we find these words: "The Spirit of the Lord GOD is upon Me; because the LORD hath anointed Me to preach good tidings unto the meek; He hath sent Me to bind up the brokenhearted, to proclaim liberty to the captives and the opening of the prison to them that are bound." Isa. 61:1.

The Hebrew term which Isaiah rendered, "the opening of the prison," has the general meaning of "opening," and is applied to opening the eyes of the blind, and the ears of the deaf. Accordingly the Savior gave it this double application, in reading it, so that in Luke instead of the one statement "the opening of the prison to them that are bound" we have the two statements "recovering of sight to the blind" and "to set at liberty them that are bruised."

The whole import of the text is that Christ came to give freedom in every sense of the word. It is charged with the idea of liberty to an extent that few realize. You will be amply repaid for a few minutes of studying it closely, and for many hours of meditating on it later.

Isa. 61:1 says that Christ was anointed "to proclaim liberty to the captives." The word "liberty" is from a Hebrew word which denotes "a swallow." The verb form means "to fly in a circle, to wheel in flight," like a bird in the air. From this it is easy to see how the word came to mean "freedom" and "liberty."

We learn that the Bible idea of liberty is best represented by the graceful flight of a swallow through the air. We often use the expression, "as free as a bird," and that exactly expresses the liberty with which Christ makes you free. Isn't it a glorious thing? What a sense of freedom thrills your soul at the very thought of it!

Sin is bondage. Jesus said, "Verily, verily I say unto you, Every one that committeth sin is the bondservant of sin." John 8:34. Not only are you in bondage, but you are in prison. The Apostle Paul says, "The Scripture hath concluded all under sin, that the promise by faith of Jesus Christ might be given to them that believe. But before faith came we were kept under the law, shut up unto the faith which should afterwards be revealed." Gal. 3:22, 23. The word "concluded" means "shut up together." All sinners are in bondage, shut up together in prison, condemned to hard labor.

The end of sin is death. James 1:15. Consequently you are not only shut up in prison, condemned to hard, unprofitable labor, but you have the fear of death continually before you. It is from this that Christ delivers you. See Heb. 2:14, 15. "For He hath looked down from the height of His sanctuary; from heaven did the LORD behold the earth; to hear the groaning of the prisoner, to loose those that are appointed to death." Ps. 102:19, 20. Christ says, "If the Son therefore shall make you free, ye shall be free indeed." John 8:36.

"Free indeed." With what you have already learned from Isa. 61:1, you can easily grasp the fullness of that freedom. Imagine a bird that has been caught and shut up in a cage. It longs for freedom, but the cruel bars make that impossible. Then the door is opened. The bird sees the opening, but has so often been deceived in its attempts to gain its freedom, that it hesitates. It hops down and finds that the prison really is open, trembles a moment for very joy at the thought of liberty, then spreads its wings and wheels through the air with such rapture as can only be known by one who has been a captive. "Free indeed!" As free as a bird.

This is the liberty with which Christ frees the captive of sin. The Psalmist had that experience and said "Our soul is escaped as a bird out of the snare of the fowlers, the snare is broken, and we are escaped." Ps. 124:7. This is the experience of every one who truly and without reserve accepts Christ.

It is the truth that gives this freedom; for Christ says, "Ye shall know the truth, and the truth shall make you free." John 8:32. He is the truth, and His word is truth. The Psalmist says, "Thy righteousness is an everlasting righteousness, and Thy law is the truth." Ps. 119:142. "I will walk at liberty, for I seek Thy precepts." Ps. 119:45. From the margin, this is literally, "I will walk in a broad place, for I seek Thy precepts." This fits with verse 96: "I have seen an end of all perfection; but Thy commandment is exceeding broad." The commandments of God form an exceedingly broad place in which all may walk who seek them. They are the truth, and it is the truth that gives freedom.

"The law is spiritual." Rom. 7:14. That is, the law is the nature of God, for "the Lord is that Spirit; and where the Spirit of the Lord is, there is liberty." 2 Cor. 3:17. Because the Spirit of the Lord GOD was in Christ, He could proclaim liberty to the captives of sin. So we read the words of Paul who had been a captive slave, "sold under sin:" "There is therefore now no condemnation to them which are in Christ Jesus, who walk not after the flesh, but after the Spirit. For the law of the Spirit of life in Christ Jesus hath made me free from the law of sin and death." Rom. 8:1, 2.

The law of God was, and is, in the heart of Christ. Ps. 40:8. Out of the heart are the issues of life (Prov. 4:23); therefore the life of Christ is the law of God. When you attempt to keep the law in your own strength, you invariably get into bondage, just as surely as though you willfully broke the law. The only difference is that in the latter case you are a willing slave, while in the former you are an unwilling slave. In Christ alone the perfect righteousness of the law is found, and therefore His life is "the perfect law of liberty," into which we are told to continually look. James 1:25; Heb. 12:2. The law that shuts you up to certain death when you are out of Christ, becomes life and liberty to you when you are in Christ.

We have seen that the "commandment is exceeding broad." How broad? Just as broad as the life of God. Therefore the liberty, or the "broad place" in which you can walk when you seek the law of God, is the breadth of God's mind, which comprehends the universe. This is "the glorious liberty of the children of God." "His commandments are not grievous," but on the contrary, are life and liberty to you as you accept them "as the truth is in Jesus." God has not given you the spirit of bondage, but has called you to the liberty which He Himself enjoys; for when we believe His word we are His children— "heirs of God, and joint heirs with Jesus Christ."

Only the Spirit of God can give such liberty as this. No person can give it, and no earthly power can take it away. We have seen that you can't get it by your own efforts to keep the law of God. The greatest human efforts can result in nothing but bondage. Therefore when civil governments enact laws requiring you to follow a certain religious custom, they are simply forging fetters for you; because religion by law means a religion by purely human power. It is not when you try to do right that you are free, but when you actually do right. But you can't do right unless the works are worked in you by God Himself.

The liberty which Christ gives you is the liberty of your soul. It is liberty from the bondage of sin. That, and that alone is real religious liberty. It is not found anywhere but in the religion of Jesus Christ. When you have that liberty you are free even in a prison cell. The slave who has it is infinitely more at liberty than his cruel master, even if the master is a king. Who is there who does not want liberty that is something more than a name?

And now one more word of encouragement to you if you are the slave of sin and are heartsick because of your bondage, and are discouraged through the failure of your repeated attempts to escape. Freedom is yours, if you will but take it. Read again the words of Christ, which are living words today:

"The Spirit of the Lord GOD is upon Me; because the Lord hath anointed Me to preach good tidings unto the meek; He hath sent Me to bind up the brokenhearted, to proclaim liberty to the captives and the opening of the prison to them that are bound; to proclaim the acceptable year of the LORD." Isa. 61:1, 2.

What is that? Liberty has already been proclaimed. Your prison doors are already open, and you only have to believe it, and to walk out, continually believing it. Christ is today proclaiming liberty to you, for He has broken the snare, and loosed your bonds. Ps. 116:16. He tells you that He has opened your prison door, so that you may walk at liberty, if you will only walk by faith in Him. It is faith that opens the door to you when you are shut up in sin. Believe His word, declare yourself free in His name, and then by humble faith stand fast in the liberty by which Christ has made you free. Then you will know the blessedness of the assurance:

"They that wait upon the LORD shall renew their strength; they shall mount up with wings as eagles; they shall run, and not be weary; they shall walk, and not faint." Isa. 40:31.

~17~

Jesus Christ the Righteous

"If any man sin, we have an Advocate with the Father, Jesus Christ the righteous." 1 John 2:1.

Of all the beings who have lived on this earth, Christ alone "did no sin." He is the only one of whom it could be said, "There is no unrighteousness in Him." Ps. 92:15. He Himself without egotism declared Himself to be sinless. And the reason why He could do this, was that He was indeed God. "In the beginning was the Word, and the Word was with God, and the Word was God." "And the Word became flesh and dwelt among us." John 1:1, 14. Christ was God manifest in the flesh, so that His name was Emmanuel—"God with us." Matt. 1:23.

Because "in Him there is no sin," "He was manifested to take away our sins." 1 John 3:5. "This is His name whereby He shall be called, THE LORD OUR RIGHTEOUSNESS." Jer. 23:6. Note that He is your righteousness, and not simply a substitute for righteousness that you don't have. Some teach that justification by faith means you are considered just without really being just. But the Bible teaches that you are actually to be righteous through the merits of Jesus Christ.

More and more it is believed by professed teachers of Christianity, that there is in us at least as much good as evil, and that the good in people will eventually gain the complete victory over the evil. But the Bible teaches that "There is none righteous, no, not one." Christ, who "knew what was in man," declared that "out of the heart of men proceed evil thoughts, adulteries, fornications, murders, thefts, covetousness, wickedness, deceit, lasciviousness, an evil eye, blasphemy, pride, foolishness."

Mark 7:21, 22. He also declared that "an evil man, out of the evil treasure of his heart, brings forth that which is evil," and that good cannot come from a bad source. Luke 6:43, 45. Therefore it is plain that from you of yourself "no good thing" can come. "Who can bring a clean thing out of an unclean? Not one." Job 14:4.

God does not propose to try to bring goodness out of evil, and He will never call evil good. What He proposes to do is to create a new heart in you, so that good can come from it. "For we are His workmanship, created in Christ Jesus unto good works, which God hath before ordained, that we should walk in them." Eph. 2:10.

You can't understand how Christ can dwell in your heart, so that righteousness will flow from it, instead of sin, any more than you can understand how Christ the Word who was before all things, and who created all things, could come to earth and be born as a man. But as surely as He dwelt in the flesh once, He can do it again, and whosoever confesses that "Jesus Christ is come in the flesh, is of God."

"If we walk in the light as He is in the light, … the blood of Jesus Christ His Son cleanseth us from all sin." 1 John 1:7. "We walk by faith, and not by sight." By faith you receive Christ, and to those who thus receive Him He gives the right and power to be called the children of God. John 1:12. Then the exhortation is, "As ye have therefore received Christ Jesus the Lord, so walk ye in Him." Col. 2:6. This is walking in the light.

As your physical life is sustained by breathing and eating, so your spiritual life is sustained by faith. Just as you cannot breathe enough today for tomorrow, but must keep breathing all the time, so you cannot have faith today for the future, but must continue to have faith. Then you can continually live a spiritual life.

While you thus walk in the light by faith, you are continually receiving a divine life into your soul, for the light is life. And the life continually received, continually cleanses your soul from sin. The cleansing is an ever present work, showing an ever present need. Thus it is that you can never say that you have no sin. It is always only "Jesus Christ the righteous."

It is by the obedience of One that many are made righteous. What a wonder! Only one—Christ—obeys, but many are really made righteous. The apostle Paul said: "I am crucified with

53

Christ; nevertheless I live; yet not I, but Christ liveth in me; and the life which I now live in the flesh I live by the faith of the Son of God, who loved me, and gave Himself for me." Gal. 2:20. So then, if anyone asks you, "Are you without sin?" you can only reply, "Not I, but Christ." "Do you keep the commandments?" "Not I, but Christ." Imperfect and sinful in yourself, and yet "complete in Him."

With God is the "fountain of life." Ps. 36:9. Christ is the manifestation of God, and so the fountain of life is in Him. "He ever liveth," and so the fountain ever flows. As it is said of the river of life, "everything shall live whither the river cometh" (Eze. 47:9), so of the life of Christ, wherever it comes it cleanses from all defilement. And so, while confessing yourself to be sinful and helpless, you are constrained to place all dependence in Him who "knew no sin," and you are "made the righteousness of God in Him." 2 Cor. 5:21.

~18~

Justification by Faith

"Whatsoever is not of faith is sin." Rom. 14:23.

Faith is of God and not of ourselves (Eph. 2:8); therefore whatsoever is not of God is sin.

Whatsoever is of God is righteousness: faith is the gift of God: and whatsoever is of faith is therefore righteousness, as certainly as "whatsoever is not of faith is sin."

Jesus Christ is the Author and Finisher of faith (Heb. 12:2), and the word of God is the channel through which it comes and the means by which it operates. For "faith cometh by hearing, and hearing by the word of God." Rom. 10:17. Where there is no word of God there can be no faith.

The word of God is the most substantial and the most powerful thing in the universe. It is the means by which all things were produced. It carries in itself creative power. For "by the word of the LORD were the heavens made, and all the host of them by the breath of His mouth." "For He spake and it was; He commanded and it stood fast." Ps. 33:6, 9. And when this world was thus made, and darkness covered the deep, "God said, Let there be light: And there was light."

The word of God is self-fulfilling, and of itself it accomplishes the will of God in you as you receive it as it is in truth the word of God. "When ye received the word of God which ye heard of us, ye received it not as the word of men, but as it is in truth the word of God, which effectually worketh also in you that believe." 1 Thess. 2:13. Thus to receive the word of God; to yield your heart to it that it may work in your life; this is genuine belief, this is true faith. This is the faith by which you can be justified, made righteous indeed. For by it the very will of God, as expressed in His own word, is accomplished in your life by the creative word of Him who has spoken. This is the work of faith. This is the righteousness—the right doing—of God which is by faith. Thus "It is God that worketh in you, both to will and to do of His good pleasure." Thus the character, the righteousness, of God is manifested in your life, delivering you from the power of sin, to the saving of your soul in righteousness.

This is justification by faith alone. This is justification by faith, without works. And faith being the gift of God, coming by the word of God, and itself working in you the works of God, needs none of your sinful work to make it good and acceptable to God. Faith itself works in you that which is good, and is sufficient of itself to fill all your life with the goodness of God, and does not need your imperfect effort to give it merit.

This faith is not dependent on you for "good works"; instead it gives the "good works" to you. The expression is not "faith and works;" but "faith which works," "for in Jesus Christ neither circumcision availeth anything, nor uncircumcision; but faith which worketh by love." Gal. 5:6. "Seest thou how faith wrought?" James 2:22. "Remembering without ceasing your work of faith;" "and the work of faith with power." 1 Thess. 1:3; 2 Thess. 1:11. And, "This is the work of God, that ye believe on Him whom He hath sent." John 6:29. This is "the faith of God" which Jesus exhorts us to have (Mark 11:22, margin); which was revealed in Him; and which by His grace is a free gift to you and every other soul on earth.

~19~

The Healing Touch

One of the most striking miracles of Jesus is told in the following few words:

"And it came to pass when He was in a certain city, behold a man full of leprosy; who seeing Jesus, fell on his face, and besought Him, saying, Lord, if Thou wilt, Thou canst make me clean. And He put forth His hand, and touched him, saying, I will; be thou clean. And immediately the leprosy departed from him." Luke 5:12, 13.

Leprosy was one of the most loathsome and dreaded diseases known to the people. The leper was an outcast, compelled to keep away from even his own family. The disease was a slow, progressive death; the victim's body becoming increasingly deformed until death ended his misery.

No other disease more aptly illustrates the defilement of sin; and this man, who was full of leprosy, very closely resembled the description given of the people, by the prophet Isaiah: "The whole head is sick, and the whole heart faint, from the sole of the foot even unto the head, there is no soundness in it; but wounds and bruises, and putrefying sores; they have not been closed, neither bound up, neither mollified with ointment." So as you study the miracle of the cleansing of the leper, you can learn how to obey the direction, "Be thou clean."

In the first place, the leper had confidence in the power of the Lord to heal him. He said, "Thou canst make me clean." That is a great point. Very few really believe that Jesus Christ can cleanse them from sin. They will admit that He can save from sin in general—that He can save others—but they are not convinced that He can save them. Let such learn a lesson from the power of the Lord. Hear what the prophet Jeremiah said by inspiration of the Holy Spirit: "Ah Lord GOD! behold Thou hast made the heavens and the earth by Thy great power and stretched out arm, and there is nothing too hard for Thee." Jer. 32:17.

He who brought the heavens and the earth into existence by the power of His word, can do all things. "Our God is in the heavens; He hath done whatsoever He hath pleased." Ps. 115:3. "His Divine power hath given unto us all things that pertain unto life and godliness." 2 Peter 1:3. "He is able also to save unto the uttermost them that come unto God by Him." Heb. 7:25. Christ has been given "power over all flesh." John 17:2.

So much for His power! Of that the leper was assured; but he was not sure that the Lord was willing to cleanse him. He said, "Lord, if Thou wilt, Thou canst make me clean." You don't need to be hesitant like that. You know that He can, and He has given you ample assurance of His willingness. You read that Christ "gave Himself for our sins, that He might deliver us from this present evil world, according to the will of God and our Father." Gal. 1:4. It is the will of God that you should be sanctified. 1 Thess. 4:3.

Christ comprises everything. He is "the power of God, and the wisdom of God." 1 Cor. 1:24. All things in heaven and in earth are in Him. Col. 1:16, 17. Therefore the Apostle Paul says: "He that spared not His own Son, but delivered Him up for us all, how shall He not with Him also freely give us all things?" Rom. 8:32. The willingness of God to cleanse you from sin, is shown in the gift of His only begotten Son for that purpose.

"These things have I written unto you, that ye may know that ye have eternal life, even unto you that believe on the name of the Son of God. And this is the boldness which we have toward Him, that if we ask anything according to His will, He heareth us; and if we know that He heareth us, whatsoever we ask, we know that we have the petitions which we have asked of Him." 1 John 5:13-15. R.V. So we may "come boldly unto the throne of grace, that we may obtain mercy, and find grace to help in time of need" (Heb. 4:16), knowing that "if we confess our sins, He is faithful and just to forgive us our sins, and to cleanse us from all unrighteousness."

But the most striking feature of this miracle is the fact that Jesus touched the leper. There was not another person in all the land, who would have come within a yard of him. But Jesus "put forth His hand, and touched him." With that touch the hateful disease vanished.

It is worth noting that in very many cases Jesus touched those whom He healed. When Peter's wife's mother lay sick of a fever, Jesus "touched her hand, and the fever left her." Matt. 8:15. That same evening, "all they that had any sick with divers diseases brought them unto Him; and He laid His hands on every one of them, and healed them." Luke 4:40. In His own country the people were so unbelieving that "He could there do no mighty work, save that He laid His hands on a few sick folk, and healed them." Mark 6:5.

In Matthew we are assured that this healing of the sick was "that it might be fulfilled which was spoken by Isaiah the prophet, saying, Himself took our infirmities, and bare our diseases." Matt. 8:17, R.V. You know that healing went from Him to the suffering ones who thronged about Him to touch Him (Luke 6:19); and this Scripture assures you that He received into His own person their diseases, in exchange for His healing power.

Now you have the blessed assurance that although He has "passed into the heavens," He has not lost His sympathy with you, but is still "touched with the feeling of our infirmities." He comes close to you in pity, because "He knoweth our frame; He remembereth that we are dust." In all your sin and degradation, you may have the inspiring thought that Jesus does not despise you, and is not ashamed to come into the closest companionship with you, in order that He may help you.

The prophet, speaking of God's dealing with ancient Israel, said, "In all their afflictions He was afflicted." Isa. 63:9. It is still the same now. As an eagle bears her young on her wings, so the Lord puts Himself under you, bearing all your sin and sorrow. He takes it on Himself, and in Him it is lost, by the same process by which at the last "He will swallow up death in victory."

Christ took on Himself the curse, in order that the blessing might come on us. Gal. 3:13, 14. Although He knew no sin, He was made to be sin for you, that you might be made the righteousness of God in Him. 2 Cor. 5:21. He suffered the death

59

to which you were doomed, that you might share His life. And this exchange is made when you come into touch with Him, by confessing that "Jesus Christ is come in the flesh." How much you lose by holding Jesus off as a stranger, or by regarding faith in Him as a theory. When you know that He identifies Himself with you in your fallen condition, taking on Himself, and from you, your infirmities, how precious becomes the assurance, "Lo, I am with you alway, even unto the end of the world."

~20~

The Power of the Spirit

Just before the Lord ascended to heaven, He said to His disciples, "Ye shall receive power, after that the Holy Ghost is come upon you; and ye shall be witnesses unto Me both in Jerusalem, and in all Judaea, and in Samaria, and unto the uttermost parts of the earth." Acts 1:8.

This promise is to you as well as to those who heard His voice as He said it; for when you know the Lord you are to be a witness for Him, and nothing can be done without the power of the Holy Spirit. God has promised the Spirit to you if you desire it and if you are willing to undergo all that is necessary to receive the Spirit.

The marginal reading of the text quoted above is, "Ye shall receive the power of the Holy Ghost coming upon you." The question is, how is this power to be received? What are you to expect and pray for? One thing may be definitely answered, and that is that the Spirit will not come to you in the way that you may have marked out. For the thoughts of God and the power of God are not after the model of your mind.

When the word of the Lord found Elijah in the wilderness, as he fled from Jezebel, it said to him: "Go forth, and stand upon the mount before the LORD. And, behold, the LORD passed by, and a great and strong wind rent the mountains, and brake in pieces the rocks before the LORD; but the LORD was not in the wind; and after the wind an earthquake; but the LORD was not in the earthquake; and after the earthquake a fire; but the LORD was not in the fire; and after the fire a still small voice. And it was so, when Elijah heard it that he wrapped his face in his mantle, and went out, and stood in the entering in of the cave. And, behold, there came a voice unto him, and said, What doest thou here, Elijah?" 1 Kings 19:11-13.

Except for the direct declaration to the contrary, you would say that the Lord was in the wind and the earthquake. It is natural for you to suppose that nothing less than a hurricane could reveal the power of God; but from the experience of Elijah you learn that God shows his power in more quiet ways. It was a voice, "a still, small voice," that revealed the Lord to Elijah. So it will be with you.

God says to you: "Be still, and know that I am God." Ps. 46:10. It is "in quietness and confidence" that your strength lies; in returning and rest you find salvation. You must be silent before the Lord, or else you will miss the still, small voice which alone reveals Him to the soul. God could thunder with a terrible voice, but you could not understand the thunder. It would only startle and terrify you. So He reveals Himself to you in a whisper that conveys intelligible sound to your understanding. We read, "How small a whisper do we hear of Him! But the thunder of His power who can understand?" Job 26:14, ASV.

Jesus was on the sea of Galilee with His disciples when "there arose a great tempest in the sea, insomuch that the ship was covered with the waves." The disciples were terrified and appealed to the Master. "And He arose, and rebuked the wind, and said unto the sea, Peace, be still. And the wind ceased, and there was a great calm." Matt. 8:24; Mark 4:39. Do you imagine that Jesus lifted His voice above the roar of the tempest in order to calm it? You cannot imagine such a thing. Only the weak man—conscious of his weakness—raises his voice in giving commands. The loud voice is used to try to conceal the lack of real power. The man who has authority, and who knows that he has the power to back up his commands, uses a quiet voice. Jesus always spoke as One that had authority; so in stilling the tempest we find the same "still, small voice" which Elijah heard.

This still, small voice is the same voice by which the universe was created. "By the word of the LORD were the heavens made; and all the host of them by the breath of His mouth." Ps. 33:6. Was it necessary for God to utter His voice in thunder, in order to bring the worlds into existence? Certainly not; an order from the commander of an army, given in a whisper, is just as effective in setting troops in motion, as an order shouted at the top of his voice. So with the King of the universe; the simple breathing from the Lord was sufficient to create all the worlds. The still, small voice that spoke to Elijah, was the voice that created. And it is the same word of power that now upholds all things (Heb. 1:3).

Most of the great manifestations of the power of God in the earth are silent and unseen. You only know that the power is there by the results. Think of the thousands of millions of tons of water that the sun is constantly lifting up from the earth to the clouds, to send down again in dew and rain. Not a sound is heard. But you can't fill a cup of water from the faucet without much noise. The power manifested in the growing plants is beyond all human conception, yet there is no sound. A growing plant can break a rock in pieces yet it is all done silently. The heavens declare the glory of God, yet they don't ring bells and blow trumpets. God's work is so mighty that the results speak for themselves; advertisement would belittle it.

But the word by which the heavens were made, and by which they are upheld, and by which all the operations of nature are carried on, is the word of the Gospel which is preached to you. The words of the Lord are Spirit and life. The word of God is living and powerful (Heb. 4:12) and it works effectually in all who believe in it. 1 Thess. 2:13.

The Savior breathed on the disciples, saying, "Receive ye the Holy Ghost." John 20:22. It was the same breath by which the worlds were made and by which they are upheld. The power of the Spirit, therefore, is creative power, and that is in the word of the Lord. So you may know that the power of the Holy Spirit, which Christ promised to His followers, comes only through His word.

God speaks to you in His word. The word of God is the sword of the Spirit. Eph. 6:17. It is the Spirit that reproves sin (John 16:7, 8), and it does it by the law; for "the law is spiritual" (Rom. 7:14), and "by the law is the knowledge of sin." Rom. 3:20.

The first thing that the Spirit does when it comes is to convict you of sin. If you accept the reproof and acknowledge your sin then the Spirit's power is manifested in taking the sin away. It convinces you of righteousness. If you reject the reproof then the

Spirit is resisted, and its power is not given to you. As the reproofs which the Spirit gives through the word are heeded, the word abides within, and your life is shaped by it. You are then led by the Spirit. As a result of your heeding reproof, the Spirit is poured out on you (Prov. 1:23), and of course the power of the Spirit is manifested in you.

Thus it will appear that it is utter folly and mockery to pray for the pouring out of the Spirit of God, while you are holding off any reproof, or cherishing any sin pointed out by the word of God. The office of the Spirit is to lead into all truth, and therefore to pray for its outpouring means to yield yourself without reserve to every commandment of God. If you do this, God will give you His Spirit without measure. It will not be given simply for your pleasure, but it is given that you may be a witness to the Lord. The pouring out of the Spirit makes known the words of God, so that you may make these words of power known to the world.

But all this will be without boasting or ostentation, although it will be the mightiest manifestation of power ever known among people. The Lord says: "Behold My Servant, whom I uphold; Mine Elect, in whom My soul delighteth; I have put My Spirit upon Him; He shall bring forth judgment to the Gentiles. He shall not cry, nor lift up, nor cause His voice to be heard in the street. A bruised reed shall He not break, and the smoking flax shall He not quench." Isa. 42:1-3. That is the way the Lord works by the Spirit. He will bring forth judgment unto truth, working with such power that the nations will be amazed, yet with such gentleness that even the reed that is bruised will not be broken, and the wick that is but dimly burning will not be extinguished. It will not be the power of the tempest, but the power of sunlight and the power of the growing plant.

Therefore, the power that the Spirit gives is the power that works throughout all creation. It is the power of God's word, and it is manifested only in you as you are fully yielded to that word. God says, "As the rain cometh down, and the snow from heaven, and returneth not thither, but watereth the earth, and maketh it bring forth and bud, that it may give seed to the sower, and bread to the eater; so shall My word be that goeth forth out of My mouth." Isa. 55: 10, 11. The Spirit is also likened to water; it is "poured out" as the rain. See Isa. 44:3. The power of the Spirit in you will be the same power that is put in operation when the rain falls on the earth. Will you yield to that blessed influence? As the earth brings forth fruit, so you are to bring forth righteousness. Isa. 61:11. Therefore "it is time to seek the LORD, till He come and rain righteousness upon you."

~21~

What the Gospel Includes

The Gospel of God is not narrow and enclosed so that it can be confined by creeds, as many people seem to think. The Gospel includes everything that pertains to human life. By its provisions you are born again—created new in Christ. Consequently everything in your life as a Christian is in touch with that creative power.

For this reason the Apostle Paul wrote to his brethren in the church, "Whether therefore ye eat or drink, or whatsoever ye do, do all to the glory of God." 1 Cor. 10:31. And to the Colossian brethren he wrote, "And whatsoever ye do in word or deed, do all in the name of the Lord Jesus, giving thanks to God and the Father by Him." "And whatsoever ye do, do it heartily, as to the Lord, and not unto men." Col. 3:17, 23.

The Gospel, therefore, touches your eating and drinking, and every activity and pursuit of life, be it business or pleasure. It makes every act a spiritual act, done with a view to the glory of God.

The Christian life is a spiritual life. It is the life of Christ in human flesh—in you as you put on Christ. This does not restrict your life, or separate you from the greater part of the life of the world around you; for all things were created by God, and were intended to be used for your benefit and pleasure. It only separates you from sin.

It shows you how to rightly use all the things that God created. It reveals the spiritual aspect of all things, so that in everything God has made or ordained you can find Him, and the life, strength and peace which He gives you. It obliterates the distinction that has been set up between religion and business. It makes the service of God your business, by showing you how to serve God in all your business, and how to find in it all a higher pleasure than any the world has to give.

~22~

The Comforter

Before Jesus went back to heaven from earth He promised to send the Comforter—the Holy Spirit—to abide with His people forever, as His representative. Since it was by the anointing of the Spirit that He accomplished all His work here on earth (See Isa. 61:1-3), it is evident that the presence of the Spirit is the same as the presence of the Lord. The same instruction, counsel, and works of love that came from Christ, are continued by the Spirit.

In promising the Comforter, Jesus said, "And when He is come, He will convict the world in respect of sin, and of righteousness, and of judgment." John 16:8, ASV. "By the law is the knowledge of sin." Rom. 3:20. But "the law is spiritual." Rom. 7:14. It is the nature of the Spirit, for the righteousness of the law is the fruit of the Spirit. Therefore there is no conviction of sin in any soul on earth, that is not the working of the Spirit of God.

But while the Spirit convicts of sin it is always a Comforter. It is as a Comforter that it convicts. Few people stop to think of that. Remember that nowhere is it said that the Spirit condemns for sin. There is a difference between conviction and condemnation. Conviction is the revealing of sin. But it depends on your course after you have been convinced of sin, whether or not you will be condemned. For "this is the condemnation, that light is come into the world, and men loved darkness rather than light, because their deeds were evil." John 3:19. The mere pointing out that you are a sinner is not condemnation; the condemnation comes from holding on to the sin after it is made known to you.

Let your mind grasp the thought that the same Spirit that convinces of sin also convinces of righteousness. It is always a Comforter. The Spirit does not lay aside one office while it performs another. It does not leave aside the revealing of righteousness when it convinces of sin, nor does it cease to be a convincer of sin when it reveals righteousness. It does both at the same time, and that is the comfort to all those who will take it. It convinces of sin because it convinces of righteousness. But let us consider this matter further, and then meditate on it.

The Holy Spirit is the Spirit of God—the Spirit of the Father and of the Son. Therefore the righteousness revealed by the Holy Spirit is the righteousness of God. Now it is only by looking at righteousness that we can know sin and its sinfulness. The law, by which is the knowledge of sin, is not sin, but is the expression of God's righteousness. You may look at sin, and if you have never seen anything else you will think it is all right. Even when you know what is right, you may lose the knowledge of right by looking at sin, so great is the deceitfulness of sin. So the Spirit must reveal the righteousness of God in His law, before you can know sin as sin. The apostle says, "I had not known sin but by the law." Rom. 7:7. So it is as the revealer of the perfect righteousness of God that the Spirit convinces of sin.

It is evident, therefore, that the closer you come to God, thus getting a more perfect view of Him, the greater will be your sense of your own imperfections. You get this knowledge of sin, not by studying yourself, but by beholding God. As an illustration, look at yourself in relation to the works of God. When do you ever feel your insignificance so much as when you are by the ocean? Its vastness makes you feel your littleness. It is the same when you stand amid the lofty mountains. On such an occasion you don't have to look at yourself to realize how small you are. It is while looking up—beholding the mighty works of God—that you realize that in comparison you are nothing. The Psalmist says, "When I consider Thy heavens, the work of Thy fingers, the moon and the stars which Thou hast ordained; what is man that Thou art mindful of him? and the son of man, that Thou visitest him?" Ps. 8:3, 4.

If this is a result of being in contact with and beholding the works of God, what will be the result when considering the character of God Himself? "The LORD God is a sun." Ps. 84:11. He is greater than all the heavens. "Thy righteousness is like the great mountains; Thy judgments are a great deep." Ps. 36:6. Just as you feel your own physical insignificance while beholding the visible works of God's hands, so in contemplating the righteousness of God, you are made conscious of your own spiritual lack. The message of comfort that God sends to His people, especially for the days immediately preceding His coming is this, "Behold your God!" See Isa. 11:1-9. That means that as a necessary preparation for His coming, He wants you to know your own lack of righteousness by beholding His righteousness.

So far you have been learning that the knowledge of sin comes by seeing the righteousness of God. Now mark the comfort that there is in that same conviction of sin. Remember that understanding your lack of righteousness is caused by the revelation of God's righteousness. Also remember that the Spirit, that convinces of both sin and righteousness, is given to you. Christ said, "I will pray the Father, and He shall give you another Comforter, that He may abide with you forever; even the Spirit of truth; whom the world cannot receive, because it seeth Him not, neither knoweth Him; but ye know Him; for He dwelleth with you, and shall be in you." John 14:16, 17.

What necessarily follows from this? Just this, that as you accept the Spirit, which, by its revelation of the righteousness of God, convicts your soul of sin, and you allow it to abide with you, then you get the righteousness which it brings. Your sense of need is itself the promise of supply. It is God who produces your sense of a lack of righteousness, which is conviction of sin. But He does not do this in order to taunt you, and cause you to despair. He does it for the purpose of letting you know that He has what will abundantly supply all that is lacking. In fact, it is by the very bringing of the supply of righteousness, that you know yourself to be sinful. Therefore, if you will take God exactly at His word you do not need to be under condemnation for a single minute, although always conscious of your own imperfections. As every new defect is pointed out, you may cry, "O Lord, I thank Thee that Thou hast this new thing to give me, and I take it as freely as Thou dost give it." This is true rejoicing in the Lord.

This is the truth that God was trying to teach ancient Israel, when He spoke His law from Sinai, and is what He has been anxious for us to learn all these years. The law was ordained "in the hands of a Mediator." Gal. 3:19. That is, in the hands of Christ, for He is the "one Mediator between God and man." 1 Tim. 2:5. He is Mediator because He reconciles you to God. Since the conflict consists of the fact that you are not subject to the law of God, the reconciliation consists of putting that law in your heart and mind. So Christ is the Mediator because He is the medium through which the righteousness of God is brought to you.

This was most forcibly illustrated at the giving of the law from Sinai. At an earlier time the people had been perishing with thirst, and God said to Moses, "Go on before the people, and take with thee of the elders of Israel; and thy rod, wherewith thou smotest the river, take in thine hand, and go. Behold, I will stand before thee there upon the rock in Horeb; and thou shalt smite the rock, and there shall come water out of it, that the people may drink." Ex. 17:5, 6. This was done, and the people drank and were revived. But the water which they drank was miraculously given by Christ. In fact it came directly from Him. The apostle Paul says that "they drank of that spiritual Rock that followed them; and that Rock was Christ." 1 Cor. 10:4. The Rock which the people saw, and which Moses smote, was a symbol of Christ.

But Horeb is another name for Sinai. So the law of God was spoken from the very same mountain from which God had caused the water to flow, which was even then quenching their thirst. When God came down on the mountain, it was the very personification of Him and His law. No one could touch the mountain without dying. Yet at the same time the water which gave life was flowing from it. This water, which, as we have seen, came from Christ, is a symbol of the Spirit which is given to all who believe. See John 4:10, 13, 14; 7:37-39. Through that event God gave us a great object lesson. Although the law gives the knowledge of sin, and sin is death, the law comes to us in the hands of a Mediator, ministered to us by the Spirit; and "the law of the Spirit of life in Christ Jesus," makes us free from the law

71

of sin and death. It is thus that the commandment of God is everlasting life.

Isn't there the very essence of comfort in this? At the same moment that the knowledge of sin comes to you, righteousness to cover and take away all your sin is revealed. "Where sin abounded, grace did much more abound." Rom. 5:20. The law which convicts is spiritual, and the Spirit is the water of life, which is given freely to all who will take it. Could anything surpass the wonderful provisions of the grace of "the God of all comfort, the Father of mercies"? Won't you drink and drink again, and thus continually be filled?

> "I heard the voice of Jesus say,
> Behold, I freely give
> The living water; thirsty one
> Stoop down, and drink, and live.
> I came to Jesus, and I drank
> Of that life-giving stream;
> My thirst was quenched, my soul revived,
> And now I live in Him."

~23~

Perfection Yet Growth

"Ye are complete in Him," is the word to the believer. In the minds of many the difficulty in grasping the completeness of the life of Christ is the fact that the Christian life is progressive. You are to continually grow in grace, and in the knowledge of the Lord; but to some this seems incompatible with being complete in Christ.

When Jesus Christ was on earth as a boy of twelve years old He was perfect. But we read that He grew in wisdom and stature, and in favor with God. Luke 2:52. Complete, yet growing in grace and knowledge—perfect all the time. The plant is perfect at every stage of its growth. We admire the beauty of the plant when the leaves burst forth. It is perfect when the flowers bloom, and perfect when the fruit comes. Yet it keeps on growing.

It is not that you are to grow into grace, but grow in grace. You are not to get more and more into grace, but in grace you are to grow and increase in wisdom, complete in Him. The very statement of this fact implies that you are not complete in yourself. There is nothing good in you, but He is yours, and of His fullness have you received, and grace over grace. Grace richly abounds and fills you.

~24~

The Life of the Word

The life of the word is the life of God, for it is God breathed, and the breath of God is life. Its life and power are thus attested: "For the word of God is living, and active, and sharper than any two-edged sword, and piercing even to the dividing of soul and spirit, of both joints and marrow, and quick to discern the thoughts and intents of the heart." Heb. 4:12, R.V. The Savior said of the words of God, "The words that I speak unto you, they are Spirit, and they are life." John 6:63. Let's see what gives the word its life.

Deuteronomy 30 describes the curses for disobedience to the law, and the blessings for obedience. The people are again admonished to keep the law, and are told what the Lord will do for them if they will repent of their disobedience. Then Moses continues: "For this commandment which I command thee this day, it is not hidden from thee, neither is it far off. It is not in heaven, that thou shouldest say, Who shall go up for us to heaven, and bring it unto us, that we may hear it, and do it? Neither is it beyond the sea, that thou shouldest say, Who shall go over the sea for us, and bring it unto us, that we may hear it, and do it? But the word is very nigh unto thee, in thy mouth, and in thy heart, that thou mayest do it." Deut 30:11-14.

Now carefully compare with this passage the words of the apostle Paul in Rom. 10:6-10: "But the righteousness which is of faith speaketh on this wise, Say not in thine heart, Who shall ascend into heaven? (that is, to bring Christ down from above); Or, Who shall descend into the deep? (that is, to bring up Christ again from the dead), But what saith it? The word is nigh thee, even in thy mouth, and in thy heart; that is, the word of faith, which we preach; that if thou shalt confess with thy mouth the Lord Jesus, and shalt believe in thine heart that God hath raised him from the dead, thou shalt be saved. For with the heart man believeth unto righteousness; and with the mouth confession is made unto salvation."

If you read this carefully you will readily see that the second passage is a quotation of the first, with additions in parentheses. These additions are comments made by the Holy Spirit. They tell you just what Moses meant by the word "commandment."

In Romans, the Holy Spirit has made clearer what was meant in the first passage. Notice that bringing the commandment down from heaven is shown to be the same as bringing Christ down from above, and bringing the commandment from the deep is the same as bringing Christ up from the dead.

What is shown by this? Nothing more nor less than that the commandment, the law—the entire word of the Lord—is identical with Christ. Do not misunderstand. It doesn't mean that Christ is nothing more than the letters and words and sentences that we read in the Bible. Far from it. The fact is that if you read the Bible, and find nothing but mere words, such as you may find in any other book, you didn't find the real word at all. What is meant is that the real word is not a dead letter, but is identical with Christ. If you really find the word then you find Christ, and if you don't find Christ in the word, you haven't found the word of God.

The apostle Paul says that "faith cometh by hearing, and hearing by the word of God." Rom. 10:17. But he also says that Christ dwells in your heart by faith. Eph. 3:17. So faith in the living word of God brings Christ into your heart. He is the life of the word.

This is also shown in John 6 where we find the statement made by Christ that the words which He spoke were Spirit and life. In John 6:35 we read, "Jesus said unto them, I am the bread of life." And in John 6:51, "I am the living bread which came down from heaven; if any man eat of this bread, he shall live forever; and the bread that I will give is My flesh, which I will give for the life of the world." And again, "Whoso eateth My flesh and drinketh My blood, hath eternal life, and I will raise him up at the last day." Then in John 6:63 He added, "It is the

Spirit that quickeneth; the flesh profiteth nothing; the words that I speak unto you, they are Spirit, and they are life." Here you find the plainest declaration that the word of God—received in faith—conveys Christ to your soul.

The only way that you can eat the flesh of Christ is to believe His word with all your heart. In that way you will receive Christ indeed, and thus it is that "with the heart man believeth unto righteousness," for Christ is righteousness.

This is a meager presentation of the theme, but who can do justice to it? You can't do more than take the simple statements of the Scriptures and meditate on them until the force of the fact begins to dawn on your mind. The fact that Christ is in the real word, that the life of the word is the life of Christ, is a most stupendous one. It is the mystery of the Gospel. When you receive it as a fact, and appropriate it, then you will know for yourself the meaning of the words that you shall live by every word that proceeds out of the mouth of God.

~25~

The Works of the Flesh

"Now the works of the flesh are manifest, which are these: adultery, fornication, uncleanness, lasciviousness, idolatry, witchcraft, hatred, variance, emulations, wrath, strife, seditions, heresies, envyings, murders, drunkenness, revellings, and such like." Gal. 5:19-21.

The flesh can't do anything good. Its works are only sin. Even when it tries to do something good, as it often does, the result is the same. The flesh is joined to sin, and there is no way in which the two can be separated. When the one is manifested, the other is manifested also. In life or death, the two must go together.

The flesh works whenever faith is absent. "Whatsoever is not of faith is sin." Rom. 14:23. When faith is present, God works; when faith is absent, the flesh works. The flesh cannot do the works that God does. The Savior declared this when the Jews asked Him what they should do in order to work the works of God. "This is the work of God, that ye believe on Him whom He hath sent." John 6:29. By faith, we receive Christ, and then the works that are done are done by Him. Consequently they are the works of God.

The great mistake which you make is in thinking that your flesh can do the works of God. Your natural mind is so ignorant of what those works are—your ways and thoughts are so far below the ways and thoughts of God—that you naturally have no conception of what righteousness is. Consequently you go about, like the Jews of old, to establish your own righteousness; and in so doing you miss the righteousness of God. You may get something that looks like righteousness to you, but if you depend on that, in the Judgment day you will find yourself terribly mistaken.

The Flesh in Bondage

When your flesh tries to do the works of God, there is manifested only bondage. Your flesh is in bondage to the law of God, for it is "not subject to the law of God, neither indeed can be." There can be no harmony between them. The Spirit lusteth against the flesh, and the flesh against the Spirit (Gal. 5:17), so that "ye cannot do the things that ye would." And this is what reveals the bondage of your flesh—the inability to do the things that it tries to do, and that God has commanded to be done. Your flesh lusts against the commands of God and is utterly unable to come into harmony with them.

When your flesh stops trying to do the works of the law, you get a sense of freedom, not because the bondage is gone, but because you don't feel it anymore. When you were struggling to walk at liberty you had a keen sense of the chains that bound you; but when you relinquished your efforts and sat down passively, the power of the chains was not felt. And if you are blind to spiritual things, you might easily imagine that you are no longer in bondage.

Your flesh is chained to sin; and whenever it tries to go in a direction contrary to sin the chains hold it back, and you realize a sense of bondage. But if you stop trying to go contrary to sin, you no longer feel the pulling of the chains. You may then, in your blindness, imagine yourself at liberty, and rejoice because you think you have gotten out of bondage into freedom. But you have no real freedom. You only have the freedom that Satan gives. For Satan holds your chains, and leads you captive at his will. So long as you move where Satan wants you to go, you don't feel the restraining force of his bonds. The devil will give you enough rope so that you will not be unpleasantly conscious of your captivity. But the moment you try to leave the path of sin and walk in the paths of God, you find yourself in bondage, and try as hard as you may, you cannot set yourself free. You find yourself joined to sin, so that you can only go where sin goes also.

By the law is the knowledge of sin. Without the law, sin is dead. Rom. 3:20; 7:8. You are now conscious of your inability to work the works of God. But when the commandment comes, sin revives. Rom. 7:9. The bondage of sin makes itself felt. To the flesh, "the law worketh wrath." It "gendereth to bondage." Gal. 4:24. It brings forth bondage, so that you feel it and realize it. "The woman which hath an husband is bound by the law to her husband so long as he liveth … So then if, while her husband liveth, she be married to another man, she shall be called an adulteress." Rom. 7:2, 3. When you are in the flesh, if you take the name of Christ, you become guilty of adultery, which is the first thing mentioned of the works of the flesh. Since the flesh is the "old man," the first husband of the "woman," then this husband must be dead before she can be lawfully joined to another. Thus when your flesh tries to work the works of God it becomes only an effort to commit adultery. Whatever your flesh does or tries to do, is of course but a work of the flesh; and if you do the works of the flesh you will not "inherit the kingdom of God." Gal. 5:21.

Some Illustrations

Abraham tried at one time to work the works of God through the flesh. God had promised him that he would be the father of many nations, and of course Abraham was anxious that the promise should be fulfilled. But as Sarah his wife was barren, he had no son. So Abraham and Sarah set about working out the fulfillment of the promise. The result was Ishmael, the child "born after the flesh," the "son of the bondwoman." Gal. 4:29, 30. In this Abraham and Sarah showed a lack of faith, for faith would have believed that God could do what He had promised, even under conditions which seemed to make it impossible. And since faith was absent, what they did was a work of the flesh, and the result was a son born after the flesh. The flesh, attempting to accomplish the work of God, simply brought bondage.

Jacob and Rebekah tried to work out God's promise for Him, when they deceived Isaac, and induced him to bestow the blessing intended for the firstborn, on Jacob. The result was a lifelong separation, with much suffering and deep repentance on the part of Jacob before he was restored to the tranquility of his early years.

Moses tried to work out the promise of deliverance for the captive Israelites by his own might, when he "slew the Egyptian, and hid him in the sand;" but that was not God's way, and he was obliged to flee into the desert to save his own life. The fulfillment of the promise was delayed forty years.

This is the result of every attempt of the flesh to work out the purposes of God. It falls as far short of what God intends and requires as the human mind falls short of the mind of God. The promise is never fulfilled, the work never accomplished, until it comes through faith.

Deliverance Through Death

God has given you "exceeding great and precious promises;" but you can never know their fulfillment through the works of your flesh. "To Abraham and his seed were the promises made;" and only when you have faith are you the seed of Abraham. In the flesh, you are bound to the "old man," the carnal nature, which is not, and cannot be, subject to the law of God; and therefore you cannot be Christ's. But you can become Christ's by being crucified with Him. You may meet Him and become united with Him at the cross. Gal. 2:20. At the cross your "old man," your first husband, is crucified and put to death, and then you can be "married to another, even to Him who is raised from the dead, that we should bring forth fruit unto God." Rom. 7:4. Your flesh cannot be separated from sin; and therefore, in order that sin may cease, it must die. You are then delivered from the "law of sin and death," the law which bound you to sin while you were in the flesh. "For when we were in the flesh, the motions of sins, which were by the law, did work in our members to bring forth fruit unto death. But now we are delivered from the law, that being dead [the law of sin] wherein we were held [because the flesh is dead]; that we should serve in newness of spirit, and not in the oldness of the letter." Rom. 7:5, 6.

This is the wonderful change that is worked in you at the cross. The law does not die, but your flesh dies, the law of sin and death is abolished. The enmity between you and the law dies; the bondage ceases, and you become joined to Christ in faith, and the law becomes to you "the law of the Spirit of life in Christ Jesus." Then the works of your flesh cease, and you work the works of faith, which bring forth the fruits of the Spirit, and you are an heir with Abraham of the promises made to him and to his seed.

80

~26~

Why Did You Doubt?

The Bible presents Jesus as "upholding all things by the word of His power." Heb. 1:3. That word not only has power to uphold, but "is able to build you up and to give you an inheritance among all them which are sanctified." Acts 20:32.

An instance of the upholding power of Christ's word is given in Matt. 14:25-32. The disciples were on the raging sea, when they were astonished by the appearance of Jesus walking on the water. When Jesus reassured them with, "Be of good cheer; it is I; be not afraid," Peter said, "Lord, if it be Thou, bid me come unto Thee on the water. And He said unto him, Come."

Peter at once responded to the word "Come," and "walked on the water to go to Jesus." Some might hastily suppose that it was the water that held Peter up; but a little reflection will show that it was not so. It is contrary to nature for water to hold a man up; and we read that when Peter "saw the wind boisterous, he was afraid; and beginning to sink, he cried, saying, Lord, save me." Jesus caught him, saying, "O thou of little faith, wherefore didst thou doubt?"

If it had been the water that was supporting him, he would not have begun to sink; for the water was just the same where he sunk as it was where he walked. So when we remember the words of Jesus, "Wherefore didst thou doubt?" We know that when Peter walked on the water, it was the word of Jesus that supported him. It was the word "Come" that brought him, and it was only when he distrusted that word that he began to go down.

The same word that held Peter on top of the water, can hold a man up in the air. Elijah and Elisha were at one time walking along together when Elijah began to rise in the air. Why was it? Because the Lord had said to Elijah, "Come;" and since the prophet had always obeyed the word of the Lord, he obeyed that word also.

We read that "by faith Enoch was translated." Heb. 11:5. But "faith cometh by hearing, and hearing by the word of God." Rom. 10:17. So it was the word of the Lord that took Enoch as well as Elijah through the air to meet the Lord. But they were only forerunners of those who, being alive when the Lord descends from heaven with a shout, with the voice of the archangel, and with the trump of God, and the dead in Christ shall rise, shall be "caught up together with them in the clouds, to meet the Lord in the air." 1 Thess. 4:16, 17.

What is it that will support those favored ones, and hold them up in the air? The same word that upheld Peter on the water. The Lord will say, "Come, ye blessed of My Father." Matt. 25:34. Those who have been accustomed to obeying the word of the Lord, will respond at once, and will be taken; while those who have not obeyed every word of the Lord, will not obey that one, and will be left.

If you have neglected to take the word of the Lord as applying to you personally, you will not accept that word, "Come," as applying to you. Only if you recognize that every time the Lord speaks He speaks to you, will you be able to take that word to yourself. The waiting ones will be those who have lived on the word of the Lord, so that at the word "Come," they will, as the most natural thing in the world, go to meet the Lord. Happy are you when you know the sustaining power of the word, and take it all to yourself.

~27~

Living Faith

The term "living faith" is strictly accurate; because faith really is a living thing. The just live by faith, and you can't live by something that has no life in it. As you can live only by that which brings life to you, and as you live by faith, it is plain that faith is a living thing.

Faith is the gift of God (Eph. 2:8) and He is a living God; Jesus is its Author (Heb. 12:2), and in Him is life—He is the life. In the nature of things, that which comes from such a source must be of itself imbued with life.

And as faith comes wholly from Him who is the only living God, from Him who alone has life, and not from ourselves (Eph. 2:8), it is certainly imbued with life, and so brings life to you by which you may live indeed.

Faith comes by hearing the word of God (Rom. 10:17); that word is "the faithful word" (Titus 1:9), that is, the word full of faith; and that word is "the word of life." Phil. 2:16. Therefore as the word of God brings faith, and is full of faith; and as that word is the word of life, it is evident that faith is life. It is a living thing and it brings life from God to you as you exercise it.

What life is it that faith brings to you? Coming as it does from God, through Jesus Christ who is the "Author of life," the only life with which it is imbued and which it could possibly bring to you is the life of God. The life of God is what you need and what you must have. And it is the life that God wants you to have; for it is written: "Walk not as other Gentiles walk, in the vanity of their mind, having the understanding darkened, being alienated from the life of God." Eph. 4:17, 18.

Jesus came that you might have life, and that you might have it more abundantly. John 10:10. "And this is the record, that God hath given to us eternal life, and this life is in His Son. He that hath the Son hath life; and he that hath not the Son of God hath not life." 1 John 5:11, 12. Christ is received by faith, and He dwells in your heart by faith. Eph. 3:17. Therefore, as only the life of God is in Jesus Christ, and as Christ dwells in your heart by faith, it is as plain as anything can be that faith brings the life of God to you when you exercise faith.

It is the life of Jesus Himself that is to be revealed in your body: "For we which live are always delivered unto death for Jesus' sake, that the life also of Jesus might be made manifest in our mortal flesh." 2 Cor. 4:11. And the life of Jesus is revealed in you, by Christ Himself living in you; for "Christ liveth in me, and the life which I now live in the flesh I live by the faith of the Son of God." Gal. 2:20. This is living faith.

He says, "I will dwell in them and walk in them;" "I will not leave you comfortless, I will come to you;" and "because I live, ye shall live also." John 14:18, 19. It is by the Holy Spirit that He dwells in you; for He desires you "to be strengthened with might by His Spirit in the inner man, that Christ may dwell in your hearts." Eph. 3:16, 17. And "at that day"—the day that ye receive the gift of the Holy Ghost—"ye shall know that I am in My Father, and ye in Me, and I in you." John 14:20. "And hereby we know that He abideth in us, by the Spirit which He hath given us." 1 John 3:24. And we "receive the promise of the Spirit through faith." Gal. 3:14.

"Christ hath redeemed us from the curse of the law, that the blessing of Abraham might come on the Gentiles through Jesus Christ; that we might receive the promise of the Spirit through faith." You must have the blessing of Abraham in order to receive the promise of the Spirit. The blessing of Abraham is righteousness by faith. See Rom. 4:1-13. Having this, Abraham "received the sign of circumcision, a seal of the righteousness of the faith which he had." And you, having this, can freely receive the promise of the Spirit circumcising the heart unto holiness and the seal of the righteousness of the faith which you have. Having the blessing of Abraham, and so being children of God, God sends forth the Spirit of His Son into our hearts. Gal. 3:26; 4:4-6. Having the blessing of Abraham, that you may receive the

84

promise of the Spirit through faith, then ask that you may receive—yea, ask and you will receive. For the word of God has promised, and faith comes by hearing the word of God. Therefore ask in faith, not wavering, "for every one that asketh receiveth; and he that seeketh findeth; and to him that knocketh it shall be opened."

Such is living faith—the faith that comes from the living God; the faith of which Christ is the Author; the faith which comes by the word of God; the faith which brings life and power from God to you, and which works the works of God in you as you exercise it. The faith that receives the Holy Spirit who brings the living presence of Jesus Christ to dwell in your heart and manifest Himself now in your mortal flesh. This and this alone is living faith. By this you live. This is life itself. This is everything. Without this, everything is simply nothing or worse; for whatsoever is not of faith is sin.

With such faith as this, that is, with true faith, there can never arise any question as to works; for this faith itself works. It is impossible to have this faith and not have works. "For in Jesus Christ neither circumcision availeth anything nor uncircumcision, but faith which worketh by love." Gal. 5:6. Since this faith is a living thing it cannot exist without working. And coming from God, the only works that it can possibly work are the works of God.

Therefore anything that professes to be faith which of itself does not work the salvation of the individual having it, and which does not work the works of God in you when you profess it, is not faith at all. It is a fraud that you are passing off on yourself, which brings no grace to your heart, and no power to your life. It is dead, and you are still dead in trespasses and sins, and all your service is only a form without power, and therefore is only a dead formalism.

But on the other hand, the faith which is of God, which comes by the word of God and brings Christ, the living word, to dwell in your heart and shine in your life—this is true faith which through Jesus Christ only, lives and works in you as you exercise it.

Christ Himself living in you; Christ in you the hope of glory; God with you; God revealed in your flesh now, today, by the faith of Jesus Christ—this and only this is living faith. For "every spirit that confesseth that Jesus Christ is come in the flesh is of God: and every spirit that confesseth not that Jesus Christ is come in the flesh, is not of God; and this is that spirit of antichrist, whereof ye have heard that it should come; and even now already is it in the world. Ye are of God, little children, and have overcome them; because greater is He that is in you, than he that is in the world." 1 John 4:2-4.

Therefore, "Examine yourselves whether ye be in the faith; prove your own selves." Jesus said to them and to you: "Have the faith of God." Mark 11:22, margin.

~28~

Judging Other People

The righteous person is the one who has the word of God abiding in the heart. And this fact is not apparent through outward circumstances. If we could look on the heart as God does, and see with His clearness of vision, we would be able to discern there either the presence or the absence of faith, and by that and that only we would know to which of the two great classes any particular individual belongs.

Faith brings righteousness. Its absence—and that alone—is the cause of wickedness. For all people are wicked by nature, having carnal hearts that are "not subject to the law of God, neither indeed can be." And the same human nature that manifests itself in murders, and drunkenness, and the lowest forms of vice and crime, is the common nature of all people. Only the accident of circumstances prevents it from being manifested in all people alike. The highly respectable member of society, who doesn't yet know God, has nothing to boast of over the person whom society brands as an outcast, for the difference between them is not a difference in nature, but merely in fortune, for which he can take no credit to himself.

When Adam sinned, he acquired a fallen and carnal nature, and that was the only nature that he could pass on to his children. So all his descendants acquired his nature, because it was transmitted by each parent in turn. And thus all people have received the fallen nature which Adam had, and only variations in the process of transmission, and in the circumstances with which they have been surrounded, have, outside of the grace of God, produced the differences in their life records. But with those who have received the grace of God, their carnal nature has been overruled. And the success of their lives has been due to this, and not to any variations of fortune. Even the Apostle Paul testified of himself, "By the grace of God I am what I am," and said, "God forbid that I should glory, save in the cross of our Lord Jesus Christ." 1 Cor. 15:10; Gal. 6:14.

Therefore it is true that those who are farthest away from God are the ones who least feel the need of Divine grace and of being saved from their sinful nature. This is illustrated by the parable of the Pharisee and the publican, who went to the temple to pray. The Pharisee thought that he had a better nature than other people, so he thanked the Lord that he was not as they were; but the publican, feeling his need, exclaimed, "God, be merciful to me, a sinner," and went down to his house justified.

The most hopelessly wicked are those who feel satisfied with themselves; and those are not the ones who manifest the greatest weaknesses and are guilty of the most crimes, but rather the ones who are able to make their lives conform to the world's standard of morality and respectability.

You may know how you stand before God, for it is a simple matter of knowing whether or not you believe His word. That word tells you to have all confidence in God and none in yourself, or in the flesh. If you say amen to this, God by His creative power makes you righteous, and you stand justified in His sight.

You cannot know the standing of others, because you cannot look into their hearts, as God does. You can only look on the outward appearance, which is not an index to the nature of the life within. Therefore the warning is given us, "Judge nothing before the time, until the Lord come, who both will bring to light the hidden things of darkness, and will make manifest the counsels of the hearts." 1 Cor. 4:5.

In Malachi we read of the time when the Lord will make up His jewels, and "will spare them, as a man spareth his own son that serveth him." This indicates a time when those who do not serve Him will not be spared. "Then," says He, "shall ye return, and discern between the righteous and the wicked, between him that serveth God and him that serveth Him not." Mal. 3:17, 18. That will be the time when judgment is given to the saints of the

Most High, and the saints possess the kingdom (Dan. 7:22) at the first resurrection. See Rev. 20:4-6.

It is not your business now to know the hidden thoughts and motives of other people's hearts. Such knowledge would do you much more harm than good. All that concerns you here is to believe God's word for yourself and sow the seed of His truth beside all waters, passing by no place because it seems to be unfavorable, but having hope for all, through the mercy and grace so abundantly given to all in the Gospel.

~29~

Righteousness and Life

Although the Gospel is a great mystery, yet it is exceedingly simple. A few easily grasped principles cover every phase. Only two things need to be understood, namely, your need, and God's ability and willingness to supply your need.

In the first place you find that you are a sinner. "As it is written, There is none righteous, no, not one; there is none that understandeth, there is none that seeketh after God. They are all gone out of the way, they are together become unprofitable; there is none that doeth good, no, not one." Rom. 3:10-12. "For all have sinned, and come short of the glory of God." Verse 23.

Sin is part of your very being; in fact, it may be said to be you. Christ, who knew what was in you, said, "For from within, out of the heart of men, proceed evil thoughts, adulteries, fornications, murders, thefts, covetousness, wickedness, deceit, lasciviousness, an evil eye, blasphemy, pride, foolishness; all these evil things come from within, and defile the man." Mark 7:21-23. These evil things come from the heart, not of a few people, or of a certain class of people, but of all people. We are told that "out of the heart are the issues of life." Prov. 4:23. So you know that these evil things are your very life. That means that your life by nature is sin.

But sin means death. "For to be carnally minded is death." Rom. 8:6. "By one man sin entered into the world, and death by sin; and so death passed upon all men, for that all have sinned." Rom. 5:12. So you see that sin carries death with it. Death springs from sin, for "the sting of death is sin." 1 Cor. 15:56. "Sin, when it is finished, bringeth forth death." James 1:15. From these texts we learn that death is wrapped up in sin. Through the mercy of God sin does not immediately cause you to die, because the Lord is longsuffering, "not willing that any should perish, but that all should come to repentance." 2 Peter 3:9. So He gives you an opportunity to repent. If you do repent your sin will be taken away, and of course you will be delivered from death. But if you refuse to repent, and show that you love sin, it works out the death that is in it. Many other texts might be quoted to show that sin means death, but these are sufficient for now. You may read these texts if you wish: John 3:36; Deut. 30:15-20, together with Deut. 11: 26-28; Rom. 5:20, 21; 7:24.

Sin and death are inseparable. When you find one, the other is there also. To save you from sin is to save you from death. Salvation does not mean simply delivering you from the consequences of sin, but saving you from sin itself. The plan of salvation is not, as some people think, a scheme by which you are free to sin as much as you wish, believing that a profession of faith will save you from the consequences of your wrong doing. On the contrary, it is a plan for utterly freeing you from sin, so it will not cause you to die. Just as you can't die without having sin, so also, you can't have life without having righteousness.

But where can you get righteousness? You can't get it from yourself, for you have nothing but sin in yourself. "For I know that in me (that is, in my flesh,) dwelleth no good thing; for to will is present with me; but how to perform that which is good I find not." Rom. 7:18. "Because the carnal mind is enmity against God; for it is not subject to the law of God, neither indeed can be. So then they that are in the flesh cannot please God." Rom. 8:7, 8. Since your whole life is sin, as you have already seen, it is clear that the only way for you to get goodness is to get another life. That is what the Gospel offers.

You are evil but God is good. He is not only good, but He is the only One who is good. Listen to the words of the Savior, to the young man who came running to ask Him, "Good Master, what shall I do that I may have eternal life? And Jesus said unto him, Why callest thou Me good? There is none good but One, that is, God." Mark 10:17, 18. This is absolute. It does not exclude Christ, for Christ is God. John 1:1. "God was in Christ." The life of the Father and of the Son are the same. John 6:57.

There is no goodness apart from God. Goodness is not a sentiment, but it is a real thing. There can be no goodness apart from actions. It is not floating around in the air like the scent of flowers. As there can't be sweetness apart from something that is sweet, and there can't be saltiness apart from salt, so there is no such thing as goodness apart from good deeds. All of God's ways are good and right. His ways are briefly yet comprehensively described in His law. "He made known His ways unto Moses, His acts unto the children of Israel." Ps. 103:7. "Blessed are the undefiled in the way, who walk in the law of the LORD." Ps. 119:1.

The law of God describes His ways and all His ways are right. His law is called His righteousness. So we read in Isa. 51:6, 7. "Lift up your eyes to the heavens, and look upon the earth beneath; for the heavens shall vanish away like smoke, and the earth shall wax old like a garment, and they that dwell therein shall die in like manner; but my salvation shall be forever, and My righteousness shall not be abolished. Hearken unto Me, ye that know righteousness, the people in whose heart is My law; fear ye not the reproach of men, neither be ye afraid of their revilings." God's law is His righteousness, and His righteousness consists of active deeds; therefore the law of God is the life of God. His life is the standard of righteousness. Whatever is like His life is right, and everything that differs from His life is wrong.

You are not left in ignorance of what the life of God is, for He lived it on earth in the person of Jesus Christ. The law of God was in His heart (Ps. 40:8), and out of the heart are the issues of life; therefore the law of God was His life.

The Spirit of the Lord was on Him (Luke 4:18), and "where the Spirit of the Lord is, there is liberty." 2 Cor. 3:17. Therefore the life of God in Christ is "the perfect law of liberty," and if you continually do it you will be blessed. James 1:25.

No other life in this world has been free from sin. People have exhausted themselves and worn out their very life in attempting to live righteous lives, and have invariably failed. We all know ourselves to be sinners. There are none who will not acknowledge that they might have done better in some things than they have done; and there are none who have not at some time in their lives said or thought that they were going to do better. This shows that they know that they have sinned. All people's consciences accuse them, even if they have not been instructed in the law of God. See Rom. 2:14, 15.

Since your life is sin in itself, and you have only one life, and righteousness cannot be manufactured out of sin, it is obvious that the only way you can get righteousness is by getting another life. And since the only righteous life is the life of God in Christ, it is plain that you must get the life of Christ. This is nothing more nor less than living the Christian life. The Christian life is the life of Christ.

But don't think that you can live this life yourself. It is evident that you cannot live another life with your old life that you have always lived. In order to live another life, you must have another life. And you can't live the life of another. You can't live the life of even your closest friend. In the first place you can't successfully imitate the things that your friend does, and in the second place, you can't know your friend's inner life. How much less, then, can you live the infinite life of Christ! You might try to pass yourself off as somebody else, but you will invariably be detected as a fraud. So it will be if you try to live Christ's life. Thousands of people are trying to live the Christian life, but the cause of their failure is that they are trying to live Christ's life with their own.

What can you do? Is it impossible to live the Christian life? No, it isn't, but Christ must be allowed to live it. You must be content to give up your sinful and worthless life, and count yourself dead—merely nothing. Then if you are truly dead with Christ, you will also live with Him. Then it will be with you as it was with Paul: "For I through the law am dead to the law, that I might live unto God. I am crucified with Christ; nevertheless I live; yet not I, but Christ liveth in me; and the life which I now live in the flesh I live by the faith of the Son of God, who loved me, and gave Himself for me." Gal. 2:19, 20. When Christ is allowed to live His own life in you, then, and only then, will your life be in harmony with the law of God. Then you will have righteousness, because you have the only life in which there is righteousness.

If you are in doubt as to how to get the life of Christ, you can read the account of His miracles, how He healed the sick and raised the dead. Read how He gave new life to the poor woman whose life was daily ebbing away. Luke 8:43-48. Read how He gave life to Lazarus and the ruler's daughter. Learn that His word is a living word, with power to give life to you as you receive it in faith. Learn that the life of Christ is in His word, so that when you hear and believe then Christ Himself dwells in your heart by faith. Eph. 3:17. Let these things be living realities, and you will surely have life through His name.

~30~

Let It Be

"Let all bitterness, and wrath, and anger, and clamor, and evil speaking, be put away from you, with all malice." Eph. 4:31. Have you read those words and thought, "Oh, that it might be so?" Have you earnestly tried to put away that evil speaking, together with "the root of bitterness" from which it springs, and failed, because "the tongue can no man tame; it is an unruly evil, full of deadly poison?" James 3:8.

Read the Divine exhortation, "Let nothing be done through strife or vainglory; but in lowliness of mind let each esteem other better than themselves." "Let this mind be in you, which was also in Christ Jesus." Phil. 2:3, 5. And similar to this is the admonition, "Let brotherly love continue." Heb. 13:1. What a blessed state of mind this must be; and what a heaven there would be on earth, if such a state of things only existed, even among those who profess the name of Christ. Yet how many who have set this blessed ideal before themselves, find themselves wondering how it is to be attained.

It is the person who is "carnal, sold under sin," who is obliged to say, "To will is present with me; but how to perform that which is good I find not." Rom. 7:18. God is just and kind. He is not a tyrant, and He does not set tasks before you without showing you the way to perform them. He not only shows the way, but supplies the power; the trouble is with the way we read His commands and exhortations. Let us read one more and see if it doesn't begin to suggest a way out of the difficulty.

"Let the peace of God rule in your hearts, to the which also ye are called in one body; and be ye faithful." Col. 3:15. Surely you cannot control the peace of God. You cannot manufacture it, and put it within your heart. No; only God can supply peace, and this He has already done. Jesus said, "Peace I leave with you, My peace I give unto you." John 14:27. "I will hear what God the LORD will speak; for He will speak peace unto His people, and to His saints." Ps. 85:8. The fact that only God can put His peace into your heart, and cause it to rule there, should indicate to you that He is the One who will fulfill those other admonitions in you.

Once more we read, "Let the word of Christ dwell in you richly with all wisdom." Col. 3:16. This, together with the previous text, tells us the whole secret. It is by the word of God that these things are to be done. "Not by might, nor by power, but by My Spirit, saith the LORD of hosts." Zech. 4:6. The word of the Lord, which sets before us these desirable attainments of thought and speech, is the agency by which they are accomplished.

What can the word of the Lord do? Read Ps. 33:6, 9: "By the word of the LORD were the heavens made; and all the host of them by the breath of His mouth." "For He spake, and it was; He commanded, and it stood fast." "And this is the word which by the Gospel is preached unto you." 1 Peter 1:25. The Gospel is the power of God for salvation, to everyone that believeth; and the power of God is seen in creation. Rom. 1:16, 19, 20. Therefore the power by which the commands and exhortations of the Holy Spirit are to be fulfilled in you is the power by which the heavens and the earth were made.

Turn to the simple story of creation. God said, "Let there be light; and there was light." Gen. 1:3. Then God said, "Let the waters under the heaven be gathered together unto one place; and let the dry land appear; and it was so." Verse 9. God said, "Let the earth bring forth grass, the herb yielding seed, and the fruit tree yielding fruit after his kind, whose seed is in itself, upon the earth; and it was so." Verse 11. And this continues through the entire story of creation.

The darkness had no power in itself to bring forth light. The waters could not gather themselves together into one place. The earth could not make a mighty exertion, and send forth the trees laden with fruit. Much less could the sun and moon, and stars create themselves. That which did not exist could not bring itself into existence. But at the word of God, saying, "Let there be," everything came into being. The words, "Let there be" carried with them the power of being. The thing created was in the word which created it.

Now "we are His workmanship, created in Christ Jesus unto good works, which God hath before prepared that we should walk in them." Eph. 2:10, margin. And "it is God which worketh in you both to will and to do of His good pleasure." Phil. 2:13. You are to remember that the commands that you read at first are not the commands of a person, but that they are the words of God to you. The same One that in the beginning said, "Let there be light," and "Let the earth bring forth grass," says to us, "Let all bitterness and wrath ... be put away from you." Just as the first was done, so will the other be accomplished. "For as the earth bringeth forth her bud, and as the garden causeth the things that are sown in it to spring forth; so the LORD God will cause righteousness and praise to spring forth before all the nations." Isa. 61:11. Therefore when you read the admonitions to let certain evil things be put away from you, and to let certain graces appear, you are not to regard them as commands for you to put them away, but as the agency by which the task is to be accomplished.

God's power to create is as great now as it ever was. He who in the beginning caused the ground to bring forth fruit, and who made a perfect man of the dust of the ground, can take these earthen vessels and make them "to the praise of the glory of His grace." You are to become so familiar with the fact that God is Creator, that when He says, "Let this be done," you will at once and continually respond, "Amen, even so, let it be done, Lord Jesus;" and thus the new heart will be created, from which will proceed thoughts and words acceptable in His sight.

~31~

Saved by His Life

The death of Christ reconciles the believing sinner to God. You are by nature the enemy of God, and this hatred consists in lack of obedience to His law. Rom. 8:7. God's law is His life, and His life is peace. Therefore Christ is your Peace, because in Him you are made the righteousness of God and are conformed to His life. In laying down His life, Christ gives it to everyone who will accept it. When you accept it you can say, "I am crucified with Christ; nevertheless I live, yet not I, but Christ liveth in me." You are reconciled to God, because you have His life. You have simply made an exchange, giving up your life to Christ, and taking His life instead.

When Christ gives Himself to you, He gives His whole life. You get His life as an infant, as a child, as a youth, and as an adult. When you acknowledge that your whole life has been nothing but sin, and you willingly give it up for Christ's sake, you make a complete exchange, and have Christ's life from infancy up to adulthood, in the place of your own. So you will necessarily be counted just before God. You are justified, not because God has consented to ignore your sins because of your faith, but because God has made you righteous—a doer of the law—by giving you His own righteous life.

You "have redemption through His blood, even the forgiveness of sins." Col. 1:14. This shows that when you receive Christ's life in place of your sinful life then you have forgiveness of your sins. "It is the blood that maketh an atonement for the soul," "For the life of the flesh is in the blood." Lev. 17:11. So you have redemption through the blood of Christ and are reconciled to God by His death, because in His death He gives you His life.

When you receive His life by faith you stand before God as though you had never sinned. The law scrutinizes you, and can find nothing wrong, because your old life is gone, and the life that you now have—the life of Christ—has never done anything wrong. But what about the future? As you have been reconciled to God by the death of His Son, so now you are to be saved by His life which He gave you in His death. How do you retain His life? Just as you received it. "As ye have therefore received Christ Jesus the Lord, so walk ye in Him." Col. 2:6. How did you receive Him? By faith. So you are to retain His life by faith, "for the just shall live by faith." Faith in Christ supplies spiritual life just as surely as eating nourishing food supplies physical life. The Savior says to you, "Whoso eateth My flesh, and drinketh My blood, hath eternal life; and I will raise him up at the last day. For My flesh is meat indeed, and My blood is drink indeed." John 6:54, 55. You eat His flesh, by feeding on His word (verse 63), for it is written that you shall live "by every word that proceedeth out of the mouth of God."

"Saved by His life." What will the nature of that life be? It will be without sin, "for in Him is no sin." 1 John 3:5. "Sin is the transgression of the law." Verse 4. Therefore that life will be the righteousness of the law. Jesus Christ is the same yesterday, and today, and forever (Heb. 13:8), and so the life that He will live in you now will be the same life that He lived when He was on this earth two thousand years ago. He came here to furnish a complete example to you of the life of God. The works He did then He will do now in you when you accept Him, and whatever sins He did not commit cannot be committed by you as you fully live His life. Notice some of the particulars of how He lived the law of God.

The ninth commandment: Jesus is "the faithful and true witness." Rev. 3:14. He "did no sin, neither was guile found in His mouth." 1 Peter 2:22. You will speak the truth when Christ dwells in you.

The sixth commandment: "For the Son of man is not come to destroy men's lives, but to save them." Luke 9:56. He "went about doing good." Acts 10:38. He came to abolish death, and to bring life and immortality to light through the Gospel.

2 Tim. 1:10. So He will live a life of love and good will to everyone, in your soul as you receive Him.

The fourth commandment: "As His custom was, He went into the synagogue on the Sabbath day, and stood up for to read." Luke 4:16. He recognized the law of the Sabbath, saying, "It is lawful to do well on the Sabbath days." Matt. 12:12. He called Himself the Lord of the Sabbath day, because He made it. He never kept a Sunday. Therefore there is no Sunday keeping in His life, to give to you who believe in Him. His life can only impart to you the keeping of the Sabbath day. As He kept the Sabbath when He was on this earth, so He will keep it now in you in whom He lives.

There are many people who love the Lord, who do not yet know that the keeping of Sunday is not part of His life, and consequently they have not yet submitted themselves to Him in this respect. But as they grow in grace and in the knowledge of our Lord and Savior Jesus Christ, they will learn that the keeping of the Sabbath—the seventh day—is as much a part of the life of Christ as is obedience to parents or telling the truth, and they will let Him live this commandment in them also. As you let Christ dwell in you in His fullness you become the child of God, because it is Christ's life that you live; and the Father will be pleased with you even as He was pleased with His only begotten Son.

~32~

Don't Forget to Eat

"Don't forget to eat! Why, I couldn't forget that if I would try," says Ernest, "for I like to do it too well. And then, another thing, my head begins to hurt, and I feel weak and faint if I have to miss even one meal. I can't work and I can't live at all without eating, so I don't think there's much danger that I will forget to eat."

Yes, but listen a minute. Do you know that you become the food that you eat? If you eat good, nourishing food, you will grow strong and healthy, but if you eat poor, decaying food, you become weak and sickly, and finally die. Even the best bread, vegetables and fruit that you can find in the market cannot build you up and make you grow into a perfect person. It may enable you to live a physically healthy life, but it cannot make your life last for more than a few short years at most. Then its power is all spent, and your life is all gone.

God says that you cannot live by earthly bread alone, but you must also have Heavenly Bread every day. Earthly bread, like all earthly things, does not have life in itself, but soon passes away. It does not have life to give you. But the Bread of Life from heaven is so full of life that it can give you life—even eternal life. If you eat it every day, it will make you grow up perfect, like Jesus, so that you will want to do only pure, good things; and it will also give you strength to do them. You know that you don't get that from earthly bread. You try again and again to do what is right but cannot.

Will God rain this Bread down from heaven for you every day, as He did the manna for the Israelites? No, for He already sent it to you, and it is within your reach.

God says that you will find all the Heavenly Bread that you can possibly need—in your Bible! The words that you see in your Bible are not the same lifeless words that you read in other books. Jesus says that the words of the Bible are full of life—of His life. And He says, "I am that bread of life that was sent down from heaven."

Don't you see that since the life of Jesus is in those words, you can get Jesus, the Bread from heaven, just by feeding on those words? You can eat them, and make them a part of yourself, by reading them every day, and believing that they are your heavenly Father speaking to you; by loving them, and believing that by them Jesus comes into your heart.

And when Jesus is in your heart won't His powerful word, that created the earth and the entire universe, keep you from sin and strengthen you to say kind words and do loving acts? You say, "Why, how can Jesus come into my heart with His Word? How can I feed on Him by feeding on His Word?" That is a question that I cannot answer. I do not know how it can be. But you do not need to know how it is done. Jesus says that He will do it, and isn't that enough? You know that He has done it, and is living every day in your heart as you eat His words.

Oh, prize your Bible! Love it and read it as no other book. Again I say, Don't forget to eat the Bread of Life every day. You need it much more than your earthly food. Feeding on it once a week will not keep you alive for heaven, any more than eating your earthly food once a week will keep you alive for earth. So DON'T FORGET TO EAT!

~33~

Have Faith in God

"Have faith in God." These words were spoken by our Savior to His disciples when they had expressed their surprise at the sudden withering of the barren fig tree. Mark 11:22. They are no less applicable to you today than they were to the little company who followed Jesus in His walks about Judea. They are the words of eternal life to the sinner sitting in the darkness and shadow of death. They are the sum of all that God, by the various ways in which He communicates with you, speaks to your soul.

Do you have faith in God? Do you know that you have it? Are you certain that you know what faith is? The disciples thought they had faith, but in the time of test and trial they were found wanting. Faith stands every test; but that which is not faith, does not endure the test. If you have faith, you will abide unshaken in the storms and temptations of this mortal life. But if what you think is faith is only a counterfeit of faith, then when the storm beats hard your house will fall. It is all important to know now whether your house is built on the sand, or on the solid rock.

The solid rock is the word of God; and there is no such thing as faith without this word. The rock is Christ, and Christ is the Word. John 1:1, 14. That word may not seem to you to be solid; but it is. We are not used to thinking of words as being solid like rocks, but this is true of the word of the Lord. That word is as substantial as God Himself. And while the earth and earthly things will pass away, the word of the Lord will abide as firm as the eternal throne. By that word they came into existence, and by that word they will be dissolved and vanish away.

Faith is composed of two elements—belief, and the word of God. Counterfeit faith has only one of these elements; it always lacks the word. It rests on something else—some feeling, or impression, or hope, or desire, or process of reasoning, or on the word of some person. Faith accepts the word of God, no matter how it reads, without questioning. Pretended faith is often obliged to explain the word away. Genuine faith "worketh by love." Pretended faith either doesn't work at all, or works by some motive which has its root in self.

The Savior said that if you have faith you could ask whatever you wanted of God, and it would be given to you. But when you have faith you will ask according to God's will, and God will always hear such a petition and answer it; for faith always rests on God's word, which is the expression of His will. And when you ask in faith, you will believe that you receive the things you asked for, basing your belief on the promise of God. You not only believe that you have them, but you do have them, really and literally. So it makes all the difference in the world for you, whether or not you have faith. Some people know and will admit the great benefits that come from faith in other people. But through the blindness and perverseness of their natural minds, they think that nothing substantial can be derived from faith in God.

~34~

Living by the Word

"Man shall not live by bread alone, but by every word that proceedeth out of the mouth of God." Matt. 4:4. Even physically, you cannot live on something that has no life in it. Dead air is death to you if you breathe it—dead water or dead food likewise. Whatever you take in the way of food or drink must have in it the element of life, or else you cannot live on it. So also in order that you may live by the word of God, that word has in it the element of life. Therefore this word is called "the word of life."

Since it is the word of God and is imbued with life, the life that is in it must be the life of God; and this is eternal life. Therefore it is truly said that the words of the Lord are "the words of eternal life." Whenever the word of God comes to you, at that very time and in that word, eternal life comes to you. And when you refuse to receive the word, you are rejecting eternal life. Jesus himself said, "Verily, verily, I say unto you, He that heareth my word, and believeth on Him that sent Me, hath everlasting life." You have "passed from death unto life." John 5:24.

Jesus used the example of living by bread as an illustration of living by the word of God. This was not chosen at random. All the words of the Lord were definitely used to teach an all-important lesson. Physically you do live by bread—using the term "bread" as embracing all proper food. But in order that you shall live by bread, it is essential that it be inside of you. And in order to live by the word of God, it is just as essential that it shall be inside of you.

You don't believe that you can live by buying the very best bread and then looking at it occasionally, or by analyzing it, and endeavoring to solve the mysteries of its composition and how it could sustain your life. Yet thousands of people really seem to suppose that they can live by the word of God that way. Many people buy a Bible of eight or ten times the proper size, with a lot of notes of darkening counsels in it, lay it on the table, and pride themselves that they "believe the Bible." They really seem to think that in some mysterious way it will make them live. But it would be just as sensible and just as beneficial for them to buy a beautifully decorated loaf of bread of several times the usual size, and lay it on the table, but not eat any, and then proclaim that they "believe in good living."

You do not expect to live by bread in this way: and you cannot live by the word of God in this way. In order to live by bread, you know it must be taken into your mouth, and be properly chewed and prepared for the digestive process, and then swallowed and given to the digestive process, so that the life that is in it may be taken to all parts of your system. So with the word of God; you must receive it as it is in truth, the word of God; you must give it a place in your heart as the word of life; then you will find it to truly be the word of life.

In the Bible, this very idea of living by bread by eating it, is carried over and applied to the word of God. "But thou, son of man, hear what I say unto thee; Be not thou rebellious like that rebellious house: open thy mouth, and eat that I give thee. And when I looked, behold, an hand was sent unto me; and, lo, a roll of a book was therein; and he spread it before me; and it was written within and without: and there was written therein lamentations, and mourning, and woe. Moreover He said unto me, Son of man, eat that thou findest; eat this roll, and go speak unto the house of Israel. So I opened my mouth, and He caused me to eat that roll. And He said unto me, Son of man, cause thy belly to eat, and fill thy bowels with this roll that I give thee. Then did I eat it; and it was in my mouth as honey for sweetness. And He said unto me, Son of man, go, get thee unto the house of Israel, and speak with My words unto them." "Moreover He said unto me, Son of man, all My words that I shall speak unto thee receive in thine heart, and hear with thine ears." Eze. 2:8–3:4,10.

Before the prophet could speak the word of God to others, he had to find it to be the word of God to himself. Before he could convey it as the word of life to others, he had to know it as the word of life to himself. In order for him to do this, he was commanded to eat it, swallow it, and fill himself with it. He was to hear it and receive it in his heart. This instruction is to you so you can live by the life of God. When you take the name of Christ you are directed to "hold forth the word of life;" but it must be life to you in your inner being before you can share it as the word of life to others.

This same thought is expressed in another place. "Thy words were found, and I did eat them; and Thy word was unto me the joy and rejoicing of mine heart." Notice that this does not say, I ate the chapters or I ate the verses, or even, I ate the subjects. No, it says, "Thy words were found, and I did eat them"—the words. Here is where thousands miss the real benefit of the word of God. They try to grasp too much at once, and so really get nothing. Words are nothing to you if you don't get the real thoughts that they are trying to express. And the greater the mind of the one speaking, the deeper are the thoughts that are expressed, even in the simplest words. The mind of the One speaking in the Bible is infinite; and the thoughts expressed in simple words are of eternal depth because they are the revelation of "the eternal purpose, which He purposed in Christ Jesus our Lord."

With your small and finite mind you are not capable of quickly grasping the thoughts taught in many of the words of the Bible. You are not capable of comprehending the words of a whole chapter, or even of a whole verse at a time. One word at a time of the words of God, is as much as your mind is capable of considering with profit.

Certainly anyone who professes to receive the words of the Bible as the word of the eternal God, expressing His thought in His eternal purpose, would have to have a good deal of conceit of his own powers of mind to think himself capable of grasping at once the thought of many of those words.

"Be not wise in your own conceits." "Be not high-minded." Do not think it too small a thing for you to take one word of God at a time, and consider it carefully, and meditate on it prayerfully, and receive it into your heart as the word of life to you. Receive it this way, and you will find that the word will indeed be to you the word of life and will bring constant joy and rejoicing to your heart. Don't think this too slow a way of getting through the Bible, or through a book or chapter of the Bible. In this way you will get through it to infinitely better advantage than to read through it quickly without understanding it. In this way you get every word, and every word that you get is eternal life to you. For Jesus said that man shall live "by every word that proceedeth out of the mouth of God." There is life in every word, and as certainly as you receive a word of it into your mind and heart, in that word and by that word you have eternal life.

Look again at the words of Jesus: "Man shall not live by bread alone, but by every word that proceedeth out of the mouth of God." How do you live physically by eating bread? Is it by gulping great chunks or whole slices at a time? You know it isn't. And you know that if you attempt to live by eating bread that way, you won't live very long at all. You know that in living by bread, you do it by taking a bite at a time.

So when Jesus used this illustration and the phrase, "every word of God", wasn't He intending to teach you that one word of God at a time is the way to live by it, just as one bite of bread at a time is the way you live by bread? Isn't this same lesson taught in the scripture, "Thy words were found, and I did eat them"?

"Son of man, ... eat that I give thee." Eat the word of God. Eat "every word that proceedeth out of the mouth of God." Then you will live a healthy and strong spiritual life just as by eating the best food, you live a healthy and strong physical life. Eat the bread of heaven and it will bring you the life of heaven; just as eating the bread of earth brings you physical life.

~35~

Prayer

Prayer is the channel of your soul's communion with God. Through it your faith ascends to God and His blessings descend to you. The prayers of the saints ascend as incense before God. They actually come into His presence. Ps. 141:2; Rev. 5:8; 8:3, 4. Prayer is the index of the soul's spirituality. There is "the prayer of faith," spoken of by James, and there is also the wavering prayer, mentioned by James. There is "the effectual, fervent prayer," which "availeth much," and there is also the cold, formal prayer, which avails nothing. Your prayers show the exact measure of your spirituality.

By faith, the effectual prayer takes hold on the word of God. Faith not only believes that God is, but that He is a rewarder of them that diligently seek Him. Heb. 11:6. It is not offered formally, but with a sense of need; not doubtingly nor despairingly, but with full confidence that it is heard, and will receive an answer in due time.

The effectual prayer is not argumentative, for it is not your place to argue with God. Its statements are not for the purpose of conveying information to God, or of persuading Him to do what He had not intended to do. The arguments and appeals of a finite person cannot change the mind of the Omniscient. You will not in faith plead with God for any such purpose. You will not want to persuade God to work in your way, for you believe God's statement that as the heavens are higher than the earth, so are His ways higher than your ways. Your constant prayer is, Your will, not mine, be done.

What is prayer and what is the purpose for which it is offered? It is the expression of your consent to what God is willing and waiting to do for you. It is expressing to God your willingness to let Him do for you what He wants to. It is not left for you to instruct the Lord in regard to what you need. "Your heavenly Father knoweth what things ye have need of before ye ask Him." He knows what you need much better than you know yourself. "For we know not what we should pray for as we ought; but the Spirit itself maketh intercession for us with groanings that cannot be uttered." Rom. 8:26.

God knows all the needs that you have, and is ready and anxious to supply them; but He waits for you to realize your need of Him. He cannot consistently, with the infinitely wise principles by which He works, bestow on you spiritual blessings that you would not appreciate. He cannot work for you without your cooperation. Your heart must be in a condition to receive an appropriate gift before it can be bestowed. And when it is in that condition, you will feel an earnest longing that will naturally take the form of prayer. And when this longing is felt, when your soul feels an intense desire for the help that God alone can give, when the language of your soul is, "As the hart panteth after the water brooks, so panteth my soul after Thee, O God," the effect is to open the channel between God and your soul. Then the flood of blessings can descend which God was already waiting to pour out. And it is the intensity of your desire that determines how wide the door will be opened.

You need to more clearly realize the great truth that God sees and knows everything that you need and has every provision made for all your wants. He knows them even before you have thought of those wants yourself. Your work is not to determine what must be done to relieve your wants, but to place yourself in a position where God can relieve them by the means which He has provided. You want to move according to His plans, and not set about the fruitless task of trying to make Him work for you according to some plans of your own.

~36~

Being Justified

"Therefore being justified by faith, we have peace with God through our Lord Jesus Christ." Rom. 5:1. What does this mean? What is it to be justified? Both professors and non-professors often mistake its meaning. Many of the former think it is a sort of half-way house to perfect favor with God, while the latter think it is a substitute for real righteousness. They think that the idea of justification by faith is that if you will only believe what the Bible says, you will be counted as righteous when you are not. All this is a great mistake.

Justification has to do with the law. The term means making just. In Rom. 2:13 we are told who the just ones are: "For not the hearers of the law are just before God, but the doers of the law shall be justified." To be just means to be righteous. Therefore when you are just you keep the law. So it follows that when you are justified, or made just, you are made a doer of the law.

Being justified by faith, then, is simply being made a doer of the law by faith. "By the deeds of the law there shall no flesh be justified in His sight." Rom. 3:20. The reason for this is given in the previous verses. It is because there is none that doeth good. "They are all gone out of the way, they are together become unprofitable; there is none that doeth good, no, not one." Verse 12. Not only have all sinned, but "the carnal mind is enmity against God; for it is not subject to the law of God, neither indeed can be." Rom. 8:7.

So there is a double reason why you cannot be justified by the law. In the first place, since you have sinned, it is impossible that any amount of subsequent obedience could make up for your sin.

The fact that you don't steal anything today, does not in the least do away with the fact that you stole something yesterday; nor does it lessen your guilt. The law will condemn you for a theft committed last year, even though you may have refrained from stealing ever since. This is so obvious that it does not need any further illustration or argument.

Secondly, you have not only sinned, so that you cannot be justified by any amount of later obedience, even if you were able to do it, but it is impossible for you by nature to be subject to the law of God. You cannot do what the law requires. Listen to the words of the apostle Paul, as he describes your condition when you want to obey the law: "For we know that the law is spiritual; but I am carnal, sold under sin. For that which I do, I allow not; for what I would, that do I not; but what I hate, that do I. If then I do that which I would not, I consent unto the law that it is good. Now then it is no more I that do it, but sin that dwelleth in me. For I know that in me (that is, in my flesh,) dwelleth no good thing; for to will is present with me; but how to perform that which is good I find not." Rom. 7:14-18. It is therefore clear enough why you cannot be justified by the law. The fault is not in the law, but in you. The law is good, and that is the very reason why it will not justify a wicked person.

But what the law cannot do, the grace of God does. It justifies a person. What kind of people does it justify? Sinners, of course, for they are the only ones who need justification. "Now to him that worketh is the reward not reckoned of grace, but of debt. But to him that worketh not, but believeth on Him that justifieth the ungodly, his faith is counted for righteousness." Rom. 4:4, 5. God justifies the ungodly. Isn't that right? Certainly it is. It does not mean that He glosses over your faults, so that you are counted righteous, although you are really wicked; but it means that He makes you a doer of the law. The moment God declares you righteous, that instant you are a doer of the law. Surely that is a good work, a just work and a merciful one.

How are you justified, or made righteous? "Being justified freely by His grace through the redemption that is in Christ Jesus." Rom. 3:24. Remember that to justify means to make you a doer of the law, and then read the passage again: "Being made a doer of the law freely, through the redemption that is in Christ Jesus." The redemption that is in Christ Jesus is the worthiness

112

or the purchasing power of Christ. He gives Himself to you the sinner. As you believe, His righteousness is given to you. That does not mean that Christ's righteousness which He did two thousand years ago is laid up for you, to simply be credited to your account, but it means that His present, active righteousness is given to you. Christ comes to live in you when you believe, for He dwells in your heart by faith. So while you were a sinner, you are transformed into a new person, having the very righteousness of God.

So it will be seen that there can be no higher state than that of justification. It does everything that God can do for you short of making you immortal, which is done only at the resurrection. But this does not mean that, being justified, there is no more danger of your falling into sin. No; "The just shall live by faith." You must continually exercise faith and submission to God, in order to retain His righteousness—in order to remain a doer of the law.

This makes clear the force of these words, "Do we then make void the law through faith? God forbid; yea, we establish the law." Rom. 3:31. That is, instead of breaking the law, and making it of no effect in your life, you establish it in your heart by faith. This is so because faith brings Christ into your heart, and the law of God is in the heart of Christ. And so "as by one man's disobedience many were made sinners, so by the obedience of One shall many be made righteous." The One who obeys is the Lord Jesus Christ, and His obedience is done in your heart when you believe. Since it is by His obedience alone that you are made a doer of the law, so to Him alone shall be the glory forever and ever.

~37~

Sabbath Miracles

The reason the Bible records so many miracles of Jesus is "that ye might believe that Jesus is the Christ, the Son of God; and that believing ye might have life through His name." John 20:30, 31.

The teachings of Jesus and the disciples tell you the way of life; but in the miracles which God worked by them you can see the reality of the life, and its power. Every spiritual truth from the Bible is illustrated by the miracles that were performed on people's bodies.

God gave Jesus "power over all flesh, that He should give eternal life" to all who come to Him. By His power to deliver our bodies from disease, He shows His power to release our souls from sin. "For whether is easier, to say, Thy sins be forgiven thee; or to say, Arise, and walk? But that ye may know that the Son of man hath power on earth to forgive sins, (then saith He to the sick of the palsy,) Arise, take up thy bed, and go unto thine house. And he arose, and departed to his house. But when the multitude saw it, they marveled, and glorified God, which had given such power unto men." Matt. 9:5-8.

Some of the most striking miracles of Jesus were done on the Sabbath day, and we wish to call special attention to them now.

The Man Blind from Birth

"And as Jesus passed by, He saw a man which was blind from his birth. And His disciples asked Him, saying, Master, who did sin, this man, or his parents, that he was born blind? Jesus answered, Neither hath this man sinned, nor his parents; but that the works of God should be made manifest in him. I

114

must work the works of Him that sent Me, while it is day; the night cometh, when no man can work. As long as I am in the world, I am the light of the world. When He had thus spoken, He spat on the ground, and made clay of the spittle, and He anointed the eyes of the blind man with the clay, and said unto him, Go, wash in the pool of Siloam, (which is by interpretation, Sent.) He went his way therefore, and washed, and came seeing." "And it was the Sabbath day when Jesus made the clay, and opened his eyes." John 9:1-7, 14.

By this miracle Christ gave visible proof of the fact that He is the light of the world. The blind beggar believed the words of Christ, and so received his sight. From this we may know the truthfulness of Christ's assertion: "I am the light of the world; he that followeth Me shall not walk in darkness, but shall have the light of life." John 8:12. When the blind man's eyes were opened he was able to see the light of the sun. But Christ was his spiritual light, showing that the light that the sun shines on the earth is only the light which it has received from the Sun of Righteousness.

We cannot see Christ, and it is impossible for our minds to comprehend how His life can be given to us, so that we may have righteousness and eternal life. But you do know that the sun gives light to the earth and that in its light there is life; and since the miracle of giving sight to the blind shows that this light and life come from Christ, you may also know that He can impart His life of righteousness to you. It is just as easy to believe in Christ as the Savior from sin and death, as it is to believe that the sun causes life and fruitfulness to the earth.

Sin is darkness. Our hearts become darkened when we don't glorify God as God. Rom. 1:21. Sinners have "the understanding darkened, being alienated from the life of God." Eph. 4:18. Just as Christ gave sight to the blind, so He takes away the darkness of sin and gives the light of life to all who accept Him in truth.

Healing the Infirm Woman

"And He was teaching in one of the synagogues on the Sabbath. And, behold, there was a woman which had a spirit of infirmity eighteen years, and was bowed together, and could in no wise lift up herself. And when Jesus saw her, He called her to Him, and said unto her, Woman, thou art loosed from thine infirmity. And He laid His hands on her; and immediately she was made straight, and glorified God. And the ruler of the synagogue answered with indignation, because that Jesus had healed on the Sabbath day, and said unto the people, There are six days in which men ought to work; in them therefore come and be healed, and not on the Sabbath day. The Lord then answered him, and said, Thou hypocrite, doth not each one of you on the Sabbath loose his ox or his ass from the stall, and lead him away to watering? And ought not this woman, being a daughter of Abraham, whom Satan hath bound, lo, these eighteen years, be loosed from this bond on the Sabbath day? And when He had said these things, all His adversaries were ashamed; and all the people rejoiced for all the glorious things that were done by Him." Luke 13:10-17.

This woman had been bound by Satan. Releasing her was a striking illustration of Christ's power to free from sin; for "whosoever committeth sin is the servant of sin" (John 8:34), and "is of the devil" (1 John 3:8); and "of whom a man is overcome, of the same is he brought in bondage." 2 Peter 2:19.

The woman could not lift herself up. We can truly say, "Mine inquities have taken hold upon me, so that I am not able to look up." Ps. 40:12. But, seeing the power of Christ on the infirm woman, we can also say, "Thou, LORD, art a shield for me, my glory, and the lifter up of mine head." Ps. 3:3.

The woman "had a spirit of infirmity." Christ had compassion on her and healed her. So we know that "we have not an High Priest which cannot be touched with the feeling of our infirmities" (Heb. 4:15), and we also know that His sympathy is practical. In these miracles we have a blessed illustration of Christ's power to open our eyes "and to turn them from darkness to light, and from the power of Satan unto God."

Why Done on the Sabbath?

The Bible specifically notes that these miracles were done on the Sabbath. Notice also that the need for healing was not so urgent that they had to be healed immediately. The blind man could have waited another day without special inconvenience. The woman had been infirm for eighteen years and was not in immediate danger. And neither of them was expecting to be healed, so they would not have been disappointed if Jesus had not healed them until the Sabbath was past.

But Jesus did not delay an hour. Moreover, He healed them on the Sabbath day, knowing full well that it would offend the Pharisees and increase their hatred for Him. This shows that He had a special object in doing these miracles on the Sabbath day, and that the Holy Spirit had a purpose in specially calling our attention to the day on which they were performed. What was that object?

The answer is easy. The miracles were done for the same purpose that they were recorded, "that ye might believe that Jesus is the Christ, the Son of God; and that believing ye might have life through His name."

Jesus did not do these miracles out of disrespect to the Sabbath day, for He kept all the commandments. Some have the mistaken idea that Jesus did them to show that the Sabbath may be broken in case of necessity. But Jesus did not break the Sabbath, although the Jews falsely accused Him of doing so. It is never necessary to break the Sabbath, but Jesus Himself said, "It is lawful to do well on the Sabbath days." Matt. 12:12.

Jesus was showing the true meaning of the Sabbath. It is true that He worked on Sabbath, but how did He do it? It was by His Word! Ever since the creation of the world, when the heavens and the earth were finished and "God did rest the seventh day from all His works," that He still continues to work by the Word of His power, which upholds all things.

God gave us the Sabbath that we might know that He is the God that sanctifies us. Eze. 20:12. So in performing those miracles on the Sabbath day, Jesus was showing that the purpose of the Sabbath is to free us from bondage. It commemorates His creative power and it is by this power that we are made new creatures in Christ, when we believe. "For we which have believed do enter into rest," even God's rest.

God rested when He had finished His work. He rested on His Word of power. So we find rest through work—not our work but God's work. "This is the work of God, that ye believe on Him whom He hath sent." John 6:29. But believing, as we have seen, gives us rest. The work of God gives us rest from sin, for we triumph in the work of His hands. Ps. 92:4.

So by these miracles Christ teaches you that the Sabbath, the seventh day of the week, is the crowning glory of the Gospel. Kept as God intended, it enables you to see Christ as both

Redeemer and Creator. His Redeeming power is His creative power. The Sabbath of the Lord, the memorial of creation, reminds you of the power of God to salvation to everyone that believes. It reveals to you, as nothing else can, that Christ was anointed by the Holy Spirit "to preach the Gospel to the poor;" "to heal the broken-hearted, to preach deliverance to the captives, and recovering of sight to the blind, to set at liberty them that are bruised, to preach the acceptable year of the Lord." Luke 4:18, 19.

~38~

Life in Christ

"For if, when we were enemies, we were reconciled to God by the death of His Son, much more, being reconciled, we shall be saved by His life." Many act and talk as if Christ was still dead. Yes, He died; but He rose again, and lives forevermore. We have a risen Savior. What does the death of Christ do for you? Reconciles you to God. He died, the just for the unjust, that He might bring you to God. Now mark! It is the death of Christ that brings you to God; what is it that keeps you there? It is the life of Christ. You are saved by His life. Now hold these words in your mind: "Being reconciled, we shall be saved by His life."

Christ's life was a sinless life, and therefore the grave could have no power over Him. It is that same life which you have when you believe on the Son of God. Give your sins to the Lord, and take that sinless life in their place.

The life of Christ is divine power. In the time of temptation the victory is already won. When Christ is abiding in you, then you are justified by faith, and you have His life abiding in you. But in that life He gained the victory over all sin, so the victory is yours before the temptation even comes. When Satan comes with his temptation, he has no power, for you have the life of Christ, and that life in you wards Satan off every time. Oh, the glory of the thought, that there is life in Christ, and that you may have it! The just shall live by faith, because Christ lives in them.

"I am crucified with Christ; nevertheless I live; yet not I, but Christ liveth in me; and the life which I now live in the flesh I live by the faith of the Son of God, who loved me, and gave Himself for me."

~39~

What is the Gospel?

This question is answered in a few words by the apostle Paul, in Rom. 1:16, 17: "For I am not ashamed of the gospel of Christ; for it is the power of God unto salvation to everyone that believeth; ... for therein is the righteousness of God revealed from faith to faith: as it is written, The just shall live by faith." But the answer encompasses so much that it will take all eternity to plumb the depth of its meaning.

There are two main points: (1) salvation from sin, (2) the power of God exerted to accomplish that salvation. We will briefly consider them in order.

The gospel is the power of God unto salvation, because it reveals the righteousness of God. This shows that it is the revelation of the righteousness of God, that brings salvation. It is the righteousness of God that saves from sin. Since unrighteousness is sin (1 John 5:17), and sin is the transgression of the law (1 John 3:4), it is evident that righteousness is obedience to the law of God. The following texts also show it: "Thou shalt call His name Jesus; for He shall save His people from their sins." Matt. 1:21. "This is a faithful saying, and worthy of all acceptation, that Christ Jesus came into the world to save sinners." 1 Tim. 1:15.

Since sin is the transgression of the law, then to save you from sin, from the transgression of the law, is to make you obedient to the law, a keeper of the law. Therefore the gospel is the revelation of the power of God to work righteousness in you—to manifest righteousness in your life. The gospel proclaims God's perfect law and contemplates perfect obedience

120

to it. But the power of God is required to exhibit righteous acts in your life. Your power is completely inadequate. This is easily seen when you recognize what the righteousness is, that is to be revealed in the life. The text says that it is "the righteousness of God." The righteousness of God is set forth in His law. Isa. 51:6, 7. Now who can do the righteousness of God? Who can do acts that are as righteous as those that God does? Clearly only God Himself. The law of God sets forth God's way. Ps. 119:1, 2. But the Lord says, "As the heavens are higher than the earth, so are My ways higher than your ways, and My thoughts than your thoughts." Isa. 55:9. Therefore your effort to keep the commandments of God will fall as far short as the earth is lower than the heavens.

All people are fallen. The work of the gospel is to raise you to a place at the right hand of God. But can you lift yourself from earth to heaven? You can as easily raise yourself from the ground to the sun, by placing your hands under the soles of your feet and lifting, as you can raise yourself to the height of the requirement of God's commandments by your own actions. You know that when you try to lift yourself by placing your hands under your feet, you are only holding yourself down, and the harder you lift, the more your weight presses downward. So it is with all of your efforts to make yourself what God's law demands. You are only adding to your guilt, for "all our righteousnesses are as filthy rags." Isa. 64:6. That which you do yourself is from self; it is selfishness; and selfishness has no place in the plan of salvation. That which is of self is of Satan; it is wholly evil. See Mark 7:21-23. The gospel proposes to save you from yourself; therefore if you plan to do the work that God requires either wholly or in part by yourself, then you are planning to do the best you can to thwart God's plan.

Many people do this ignorantly, but the result is the same. It was because the Jews were ignorant of God's righteousness that they went about to establish their own righteousness. Rom. 10:1-3. If you realize the infinite depth and height and breadth of the character of God, which is summed up in His law, you will readily see that nothing short of the power of God can produce that character in you. Only God Himself can do the works of God. For you to assume that you by yourself are able to do

God's righteous works, is to make yourself equal with God; and that is the very "mystery of iniquity" itself.

The work of the gospel is to put God's righteous works in the place of your unrighteousness. It is to work in you the works of God, and to cause you to think the thoughts of God. It is to save you from all unrighteousness, to deliver you from "this present evil world," to redeem you from all iniquity; that is the result. By what means is it to be accomplished? By the power of God. We must know what that power is, and how it is received.

Immediately after the statement that the gospel is the power of God to salvation, the apostle tells us how we may know the power. "For the invisible things of Him from the creation of the world are clearly seen, being understood by the things that are made, even His eternal power and Godhead." Rom. 1:20. That is, God's power is seen in the things that He has made. Creation reveals the power of God, for His power is creative power. The fact that God creates is what distinguishes Him as the one true God. The Psalmist says: "For the LORD is great and greatly to be praised; He is to be feared above all gods. For all the gods of the nations are idols [nothing]: but the LORD made the heavens." Ps. 96:4, 5.

Again we read: "But the LORD is the true God, He is the living God, and an everlasting king; at His wrath the earth shall tremble, and the nations shall not be able to abide His indignation. Thus shall ye say unto them, The gods that have not made the heavens and the earth, even they shall perish from the earth, and from under the heavens. He hath made the earth by His power, He hath established the world by His wisdom, and hath stretched out the heavens by His discretion. When He uttereth His voice, there is a multitude of waters in the heavens, and He causeth the vapors to ascend from the ends of the earth; He maketh lightnings with rain, and bringeth forth the wind out of His treasures." Jer. 10:10-13.

Ps. 33:6, 9, tells us how the Lord made the heavens and the earth: "By the word of the LORD were the heavens made; and all the host of them by the breath of His mouth." "For He spake, and it was; He commanded, and it stood fast." It was made by His word. When God speaks, the very thing itself exists in the words which describe or name the thing. Thus it is that He "calleth those things which be not as though they were." Rom. 4:17. If you call a thing that is not as though it were, it is a lie; but not so when God so speaks, for His very word causes it to exist. When He speaks the word, there the thing is. "He spake, and it was."

The same word that creates also upholds. In Heb. 1:3 we read that Christ, who created all things, upholds all things "by the word of His power." The creative power of the word of God is seen in the preservation of the earth and the heavenly bodies, and in the growth of all plants. Also the words of the Lord by the prophet Isaiah: "To whom then will ye liken me, or shall I be equal? saith the Holy One. Lift up your eyes on high, and behold who hath created these things, that bringeth out their host by number; He calleth them all by names by the greatness of His might, for that He is strong in power; not one faileth." Isa. 40:25, 26.

The reason the word can do all these things is because the word of God is living. Being the breath of God, it has the incorruptible nature of God, so that its power never diminishes. Isaiah 40 is wholly devoted to showing the power of God. The word by which all these things are upheld is spoken of in verses 7, 8: "The grass withereth, the flower fadeth; because the spirit of the LORD bloweth upon it; surely the people is grass. The grass withereth, the flower fadeth; but the word of our God shall stand for ever." The apostle Peter quotes these words, and adds: "This is the word which by the gospel is preached unto you." 1 Pet. 1:25.

The gospel is the power of God unto salvation. And the power of God is shown in creating and upholding the earth; therefore the gospel is the creative power of God exercised for saving you from sin. So the apostle says: "If any man be in Christ, he is a new creature; old things are passed away; behold, all things are become new. And all things are of God." 2 Cor. 5:17, 18. "For we are His workmanship, created in Christ Jesus unto good works, which God hath before ordained that we should walk in them." Eph. 2:10. The work of redemption is the work of producing a new creation—new people, new heavens, and new earth—by the same word that created all things in the beginning.

What greater encouragement can God give you than this? The power that works in you to do that which is well-pleasing in the sight of the Lord, is the same power that made the heavens and the earth, and which upholds them! Why should there be any discouragement?

Remember that He who upholds all things by the word of His power, is "able to keep you from falling, and to present you faultless before the presence of His glory, with exceeding joy." Jude 24.

~40~

Present Tense Religion

"I am crucified with Christ; nevertheless I live; yet not I, but Christ liveth in me; and the life which I now live in the flesh I live by the faith of the Son of God, who loved me, and gave Himself for me." Gal. 2:20. "Whosoever is born of God doth not commit sin; for His seed remaineth in him; and he cannot sin because he is born of God." "Whatsover is born of God overcometh the world; and this is the victory that overcometh the world, even our faith." 1 John 3:9; 5:4.

From these texts and many others that might be cited it is evident that the Christian religion is a religion of the present tense. In the Christian life, nothing counts for anything except what is present. Whatever has been in the past is valuable only for its present influence and effect; and the same is true of that which is to come.

To be born of God is to receive your life from Him, just as you received life through birth from your earthly parents. But the new birth is a continuous process, and thus something that is ever present. It is the life from the Vine coming into you, a branch. John 15:1. Thus it is a continuous flow of life from God into you. "I am the Vine, ye are the branches. He that abideth in Me, and I in him, the same bringeth forth much fruit." John 15:5.

If religion were a thing of the past tense, you would be turning your eyes backward instead of forward; and if it belonged to the future tense, you would always be waiting for the appointed time. In either case you would not grow. This is the great trouble with many who profess to be Christians; they always look either to the past or to the future. If to the past, they measure the possibilities of their Christian life by some past experience. If they had some genuine experience in the past, they think it could not have been genuine because they later fail; and then they become discouraged. And if to the future, they wait for a time that never comes, since they can only live in the present.

Christianity in the present tense takes you just where it finds you; and therefore you don't need to wait or be discouraged. The Lord intends to save you and He cannot do this except by taking you just where you are now, and just where you are at each succeeding moment of your life. Each moment will become "now" as soon as you reach it. If He cannot save you in this way, He cannot save you at all. But He has assured you that He is able to save you, to the very uttermost, if you will look to Him.

Therefore the only thing to do is simply to look to Him now and believe now, without reference to your past failures or future hopes. The only starting point in the Christian life is "now;" the only point attainable is "now." To live now is not for you to wish or resolve or anticipate now, but to believe and take. It is looking to Christ now. It is when you forget to live in the present moment, by looking at that moment to Jesus Christ for grace and strength, that you fail.

~41~

A New Creation

True Sabbath keeping means rest in the Lord—depending on Him as the Creator, who is able to create you a new creature in Christ Jesus. This thought is worthy of further consideration. Let's recall a few plain statements of Scripture.

God has made His wonderful works to be remembered. Ps. 111:4.

He wants you to remember His wonderful works, in order that you may know His power, because His power is known by His works. Rom. 1:20.

It is necessary for you to know the power of God, in order that you may be saved, because the Gospel is the power of God to salvation to everyone that believes. Rom. 1:16. It is by the power of God, through faith, that you are kept. 1 Peter 1:5.

The Sabbath is a memorial that God gave you of His wonderful works. "And God blessed the seventh day, and sanctified it, because that in it He had rested from all His work which God created and made." Gen. 2:3. "The seventh day is the Sabbath of the LORD thy God; in it thou shalt not do any work, thou, nor thy son, nor thy daughter, thy manservant, nor thy maidservant, nor thy cattle, nor thy stranger that is within thy gates; for in six days the LORD made heaven and earth, the sea, and all that in them is, and rested the seventh day; wherefore the LORD blessed the Sabbath day, and hallowed it." Ex. 20:10, 11.

Since the Sabbath is the memorial of the wonderful works of God, and God is known by His works, it follows that the Sabbath gives the knowledge of God. And so He says: "And hallow My

Sabbaths; and they shall be a sign between Me and you, that ye may know that I am the LORD your God." Eze. 20:20.

But to know God is to know Him as He is. It is to know that He is love (1 John 4:16), that He is of great compassion (Lam. 3:22), that He is merciful (Ps. 103:8, 11, 17), that He delights in mercy (Micah 7:18), that He takes no pleasure in the death of any (Eze. 33:11), that He has interposed Himself for your salvation (Heb. 6:13-20) and that He is able to do all that He has promised. Rom. 4:21; Eph. 3:20. In short, to know God is to know Jesus Christ, "for in Him dwelleth all the fullness of the Godhead bodily" (Col. 2:9), and God is manifested only in Christ. John 1:18. "God was in Christ, reconciling the world unto Himself." 2 Cor. 5:19.

Christ is the power of God. 1 Cor. 1:24. Therefore the works of God, by which the power of God is known, make Christ known to you. This is evident enough, because "by Him were all things created." Col. 1:16. "All things were made by Him." John 1:3. And since the Sabbath is the memorial of creation, it is the memorial of the power of Christ. But Christ is your Savior. "He was manifested to take away our sins." 1 John 3:5. Therefore the Sabbath is for the purpose of letting you know the power of Christ to save you from sin. This we also plainly read: "Moreover also I gave them my Sabbaths, to be a sign between Me and them, that they might know that I am the LORD that sanctify them." Eze. 20:12.

When God had finished the six days of creation, He "saw everything that He had made, and behold, it was very good." Gen. 1:31. This look included us. "God made man upright." Eccl. 7:29. Since the Sabbath is the memorial of a perfect creation it shows the power of God to create a perfect earth, and perfect people to dwell on it.

"They shall go to confusion together that are makers of idols. But Israel shall be saved in the LORD with an everlasting salvation; ye shall not be ashamed nor confounded world without end. For thus saith the LORD that created the heavens; God Himself that formed the earth and made it; He hath established it. He created it not in vain, He formed it to be inhabited; I am the LORD; and there is none else. I have not spoken in secret, in a dark place of the earth; I said not unto the seed of Jacob, Seek ye

Me in vain; I the LORD speak righteousness, I declare things that are right." Isa. 45:16-19.

Notice carefully what this text says. The makers of idols will be ashamed and confounded, but Israel will be saved in the Lord with an everlasting salvation. Why? Because the Lord made the earth to be inhabited; He did not make it in vain. If it were not inhabited, it would have been made in vain. But He showed in the beginning what kind of people He designed to inhabit the earth. He made the earth to be inhabited by perfect beings. Now since He didn't make it in vain, it is going to be inhabited by just the kind of people that He made to inhabit it in the beginning. He is going to save people out of this earth, making them perfect, to inhabit the earth forever. He will make the earth new for their habitation. See Rev. 21:1, 5; 22:1-5; 2 Peter 3:13.

Therefore the Sabbath is both a memorial and a pledge. It is a sign that God made everything perfect in the beginning and it is a pledge that He will restore all things to perfection as they were in the beginning. He will create a new earth. What does that mean? It means that the earth is to be restored to the condition that it was in when it was first created. It was then a new earth, and God is going to make it new again. But it will be inhabited, for the Lord did not make it in vain. And it will be inhabited by perfect people. Only righteousness will dwell on the new earth.

The Sabbath reminds you that God made the earth by His power. The Sabbath also makes Jesus known to you as the One who by His power will create you as a new creature in Christ to dwell on the new earth.

So the Sabbath is the seal of a perfect creation, both in the beginning, and at the last. Keeping the Sabbath means perfect submission to the will of God, so that His will may be done on earth as it is done in heaven. It means for you to give the Lord His way with you, so that He can make you to the praise of the glory of His grace, wherein He hath made you accepted in the Beloved. Eph 1:5, 6.

The Sabbath is God's rest. It is the rest which God entered into when He ceased from His work, and left His word to uphold that which it had created. That rest He gave to the first humans in Eden. That same rest He gives now to all who will accept Him. It is the rest in which you are to be saved, as the Lord says, "In returning and rest shall ye be saved; in quietness and in confidence shall be your strength." Isa. 30:15. It is resting on the power which made the heavens and the earth, and which still holds them up. It is the rest which in the beginning was connected with the new earth, and so having that rest is the assurance of rest in the earth when it is again made new. And so it is fitting that when the earth is made new, the Sabbath will be observed by all flesh. See Isa. 66:22, 23.

~42~

A Lesson from Real Life

"Therefore having been justified by faith, we have peace with God through our Lord Jesus Christ." Rom. 5:1.

"Therefore by the offence of one, judgment came upon all men to condemnation; even so by the righteousness of One, the free gift came upon all men unto justification of life. For as by one man's disobedience many were made sinners, so by the obedience of One shall many be made righteous." Rom. 5:18, 19.

"The kingdom of God is not in word, but in power." 1 Cor. 4:20. The promises of the gift of the Gospel are not matters of mere theory, but a fact. And in order to show you the reality of the power, Jesus Christ came to earth and demonstrated it in such a way that you can comprehend it. In the life of Christ you will find every Gospel truth illustrated. Let's see something of how the above texts worked in real life.

A woman was bleeding and her life had been slowly and steadily wasting away for many years. She had spent all her income in a vain attempt to recover her health, and was only made to suffer more from the experiments of many physicians. Then she heard of the great Physician and went to Him. She was timid and the multitude of people pressed about Jesus so closely that she could scarcely approach Him. But "she said within herself, If I may but touch His garment, I shall be whole." Her faith was rewarded, for as she touched the border of His garment, she was fully healed immediately.

Although Jesus was crowded and jostled by the people, He instantly detected that gentle touch. That touch was different from every other, because it was the touch of faith, and drew power from the person of Jesus. When the disciples wondered that in the midst of such a crowd He should ask, "Who touched Me?" He said, "Someone did touch Me; for I perceived that power had gone forth from Me." That power was the power of His life: for it supplied the woman's need, and what she wanted was life.

Here you have something that your mind can understand, and your senses can appreciate. A real thing was done. Something real went from Jesus into the woman. It was not imagination; it was not a figure of speech; but it was an actual fact that the woman was healed. She had the life that she lacked before, and that life came from Jesus. You can never know what life is— only its Author can understand it—but you do know the need of it, even of the righteous life of Christ. Now you will see how to obtain it.

The words of Jesus to that poor woman show that she was healed in the same way and by the same means by which you are justified and have peace with God. He said to her, "Daughter, be of good comfort; thy faith hath made thee whole; go in peace." Luke 8:48. If you should apply the words of the Apostle Paul to her particular experience, you might read, "Therefore being made whole in body by faith, she had peace with God through our Lord Jesus Christ." Perhaps this may enable you to grasp more fully the reality of the righteousness which comes by faith of Jesus Christ.

Nothing is said about forgiveness of sins in this instance, but you may be sure from other instances that such faith as the poor woman had, brought healing of the soul as well as the body. But you don't need to doubt whether this is really parallel to Rom. 5:1, and the illustration of the truth stated there, for you find the same words used with direct reference to sins. In the preceding chapter (Luke 7) you are told of the sinful woman who anointed the feet of Jesus, after her tears of repentance had washed them. Jesus did not repel her, but said to her, "Thy sins are forgiven." And then He said words almost identical to what He said to the bleeding woman you have been reading about. To the woman who was well in body, but morally diseased with sin, Jesus said, "Thy faith hath saved thee; go in peace." Luke 7:50. Compare Luke 8:48.

This proves beyond all possibility of doubt that the same thing is done in the forgiveness of sins that was done in healing the woman who was bleeding. The method is the same, and the results are the same. Therefore as you know that something real was done for the diseased woman, so you may be sure that something real is done for you as a repentant sinner. Just as something real, although invisible, went from Jesus into the person of the diseased woman, making her perfectly well and strong, even so you are to know that something real comes from Christ into your person as a repentant sinner, making you whole, and free from sin.

That something is nothing less than the life of Christ. "If we confess our sins, He is faithful and just to forgive us our sins, and to cleanse us from all unrighteousness." 1 John 1:9. "If we walk in the light, as He is in the light, we have fellowship one with another, and the blood of Jesus Christ His Son cleanseth us from all sin." Verse 7. The blood is the life; and so it is the life of Jesus Christ that cleanses you from sin. Rom. 5:10 says in continuance of the statement that being justified by faith you have peace with God through your Lord Jesus Christ. "For if, when we were enemies, we were reconciled to God by the death of His Son, much more being reconciled, we shall be saved by His life."

Many think that the forgiveness of sins by the imputed righteousness of Christ, is something that exists only in the mind of God. Of course they acknowledge its reality, yet at the same time they do not realize it. There is always something unreal about it in their minds. The trouble is that they fail to grasp and to make real the living connection between Christ and them. There is between the true disciple and Christ a connection as real as that between the vine branch and the parent stock. The forgiveness of sins is too often thought to be illustrated by the payment of a poor man's debt by a rich friend. If a rich man pays the debt of a poor man, and the banker credits the poor man with the sum, then the record on the books shows that the debt is cancelled. Of course the poor man is benefited, but he does not actually receive anything that will keep him in the future. But it is different when God for Christ's sake forgives your sins.

Christ "gave Himself for our sins." Gal. 1:4. His life is given to be revealed in your mortal flesh. 2 Cor. 4:11. Just as the sap flows through the vine to the farthest branches, and just as the life of Christ went into the poor, diseased woman, to make her perfectly well, so the sinless, endless, inexhaustible life of Christ flows into you when you have faith in Him, to cleanse you from sin, and to make you walk in newness of life.

Christ's life on earth was one of obedience to the commandments of God. John 15:10. The law of God was in His heart (Ps. 40:8) so that His very life was the fullness of the law. He fulfilled the righteousness of the law. Matt. 5:17. That is, the fullness, the perfection of the law, appeared in His life. And it is by this life that you are saved. It is not that you are accounted righteous because Jesus of Nazareth was righteous two thousand years ago, but because "He ever liveth," "the same yesterday, and today, and forever," to save you by the power of His endless life, when you come to Him.

Jesus fulfilled the righteousness of the law, in order "that the righteousness of the law might be fulfilled in us, who walk not after the flesh, but after the Spirit." Rom. 8:4. The Revised Version reads, "That the ordinance of the law might be fulfilled in us," and gives "requirement" in the margin, as an alternative. The idea is, that Christ kept the law, in order that its every requirement might be fulfilled in you. Not by you, but in you: for you have no power to do even what you know to be right. But Christ dwelling in you does the right by His own power through all your members when you yield them to Him. This He does for all who trust Him. And thus it is that "by the obedience of One shall many be made righteous."

You may note two things. First: The miraculous healing of the poor woman shows you how you are made a partaker of Christ's life. Second: You learn what will happen as you are a partaker of Christ's life. You learn by reading the Ten Commandments, and by studying the life of Christ. All that was in His life when He was on earth, is in it now, and that is what He gives to you. And that which was not in His life cannot possibly be given to you in it. Everything that is not in His life is sin, and Christ is not the minister of sin.

~43~

Making Mistakes

The fact that God dwells in you, as He does in everyone who believes on the name of Jesus, does not preclude you from exhibiting the limitations of humanity. It keeps you from sin, but not from all the mistakes that arise from the limitations of human vision and judgment. The mystery of godliness is God in you— God manifested in the life of righteousness and you manifested in the frailties of the flesh. The one contrasts with the other, and by the very contrast it is manifest that the life is not of you, but of God; and that to Him alone belongs the glory.

~44~

Creation and Redemption

"In the beginning God created the heaven and the earth." Gen. 1:1. In this brief sentence we have the whole of the truth of the Gospel summed up. If you read it correctly, you may derive a world of comfort from it.

In the first place, consider who it was that created the heaven and earth. "God created." But Christ is God, the brightness of the Father's glory, and express image of His person. Heb. 1:3. He Himself said, "I and My Father are one." John 10:30. It was He who—representing the Father—created the heaven and the earth. "In the beginning was the Word, and the Word was with God, and the Word was God. The same was in the beginning with God. All things were made by Him; and without Him was not anything made that was made." John 1:1-3. We read of Christ, "by Him were all things created, that are in heaven, and that are in earth, visible and invisible, whether they be thrones, or dominions, or principalities, or powers; all things were created by Him, and for Him; and He is before all things, and by Him all things consist." Col. 1:16, 17.

The Father Himself addresses the Son as God, and as Creator. The first chapter of Hebrews says that God has not at any time said to any of the angels, "Thou art My Son, this day have I begotten Thee;" "but unto the Son He saith, Thy throne, O God, is for ever and ever; a scepter of righteousness is the scepter of Thy kingdom." And He also said to the Son, "Thou, Lord, in the beginning hast laid the foundation of the earth; and the heavens are the work of Thy hands." Heb. 1:5, 8, 10. So you are well assured that when you read in the first chapter of Genesis, that "in the beginning God created the heaven and the earth," it refers to God in Christ.

Creative power is the distinguishing mark of Divinity. The Spirit of the Lord through the prophet Jeremiah describes the vanity of idols, and then continues: "But the LORD is the true God, He is the living God, and an everlasting King; at His wrath the earth shall tremble, and the nations shall not be able to abide His indignation. Thus shall ye say unto them, The gods that have not made the heavens and the earth, even they shall perish from the earth, and from under these heavens. He hath made the earth by His power, He hath established the world by His wisdom, and hath stretched out the heavens by His discretion." Jer. 10:10-12. The earth was made by His power, and established by His wisdom. But Christ is "The power of God, and the wisdom of God." So here again you find Christ inseparably connected with creation as the Creator. Only as you acknowledge and worship Christ as the Creator, do you acknowledge His Divinity.

Christ is Redeemer by virtue of His power as Creator. "We have redemption through His blood, even the forgiveness of sins," because "by Him were all things created." Col. 1:14, 16. If He were not Creator, He could not be Redeemer. This simply means that redemptive power and creative power are the same. To redeem is to create. This is shown in the statement of the apostle that the Gospel is the power of God unto salvation, and the power of God is seen by means of the things that have been made. Rom. 1:16, 20. When you consider the works of creation, and think of the power manifested in them, you are contemplating the power of redemption.

There has been a great deal of idle speculation as to which is greater, redemption or creation? Many have thought that redemption is a greater work than creation. Such speculation is idle, because only infinite power could perform either work, and infinite power cannot be measured by human minds. But while we cannot measure the power, we can easily settle the question about which is greater, because the Scriptures give us the information. Neither is greater than the other, for both are the same. Redemption is creation. Redemption is the same power that was put forth in the beginning to create the world and all that is in it, now put forth to save people and the earth from the curse of sin.

The Scriptures are very clear on this point. The Psalmist prayed, "Create in me a clean heart and renew a right spirit in me." Ps. 51:10. The apostle says "If any man be in Christ, he is a new creature," or a new creation. 2 Cor. 5:17. And we read: "For by grace are ye saved through faith; and that not of yourselves; it is the gift of God; not of works, lest any man should boast. For we are His workmanship, created in Christ Jesus unto good works, which God hath before ordained that we should walk in them." Eph. 2:8-10.

Compared with God, "Man is less than nothing, and vanity." In you "dwelleth no good thing." But the same power that in the beginning made the earth from nothing, can take you if you are willing, and make of you that which is "to the praise of the glory of His grace."

~45~

The Law and the Life

The keeping of the commandments of God is summed up in one word, namely, love. But love is of God, "For God is love." Notice that the text does not say that God has love, but that God is love. Love is the nature of God; it is His very life. Therefore it is plain that keeping the commandments of God is partaking of God's nature. This is a point that cannot be too often repeated.

When the young man came to Christ, saying, "Good Master," the Savior said to him, "Why callest thou Me good? There is none good but One, that is, God." In this, Christ was not rebuking him for calling Him good, because He was good. He "knew no sin." To the Jews He said, "Which of you convinceth Me of sin?" John 8:46. And again He said, "The prince of this world cometh, and hath nothing in Me." John 14:30. He knew that He was good, and He could not deny that without denying Himself, and He would not do that. But in asking that question and making that statement to the young man, He showed that He Himself was God. He and the Father are one, and God alone is good.

In contrast with God, you are only evil. "There is none righteous, no, not one; there is none that understandeth, there is none that seeketh after God. They are all gone out of the way, they are together become unprofitable; there is none that doeth good, no, not one." Rom. 3:10-12. "Out of the heart of men, proceed evil thoughts, adulteries, fornications, murders, thefts, covetousness, wickedness, deceit, lasciviousness, an evil eye, blasphemy, pride, foolishness; all these evil things come from within, and defile the man." Mark 7:21-23.

As your heart is, so are you. "An evil man, out of the evil treasure of his heart, bringeth forth that which is evil." Luke 6:45. So since your heart is evil then you can only do evil when left to yourself. "For the flesh lusteth against the Spirit, and the Spirit against the flesh; and these are contrary the one to the other; so that ye cannot do the things that ye would." Gal. 5:17. This is spoken especially of you when you desire to do what is right.

This evil in your heart is opposed to the law of God. We read, "to be carnally minded is death; but to be spiritually minded is life and peace. Because the carnal mind is enmity against God; for it is not subject to the law of God, neither indeed can be. So then they that are in the flesh cannot please God." Rom. 8:6-8.

But God tells you to keep His commandments. And since it is impossible for your nature to keep them, and goodness resides in God alone, it follows that in order for you to keep the commandments you must have the nature of God. Christ is the revelation of God. No man knoweth "the Father save the Son, and he to whomsoever the Son will reveal Him." Matt. 11:27. In Christ's life there was perfect goodness, because His life was the life of God. God is good. His life is goodness itself. Goodness constitutes His life. Goodness is not an abstract thing, but it must always be manifested in action. But action is life. Therefore since there is none good but God, it follows that if you would keep the commandments of God you must do so by having His life in you.

This is the only way that the righteousness of the law can occur in your life. Paul said, "I am crucified with Christ; nevertheless I live; yet not I, but Christ liveth in me; and the life which I now live in the flesh I live by the faith of the Son of God, who loved me, and gave Himself for me. I do not frustrate the grace of God; for if righteousness come by the law, then Christ is dead in vain." Gal. 2:20, 21. Righteousness comes only by the life of God in Christ. So it is that "by the obedience of One shall many be made righteous." Rom. 5:19. In all the host of the redeemed in the kingdom of heaven, there will be the manifestation of the righteousness of Christ, and of His righteousness alone. It is not simply that Christ obeyed the law two thousand years ago, when He was on earth. But that He obeys the law now, the same as He did then; for He is the same yesterday, and today, and forever. So when He comes to dwell in your heart by faith, He lives the same life of obedience in you that He did when He came here to die for you. When you know this in practice you are acknowledging that Christ is come in the flesh.

It is because the law of God is the life of God, and the law is love, that the Savior gave this instruction: "I say unto you, Love your enemies, bless them that curse you, do good to them that hate you, and pray for them which despitefully use you, and persecute you; that ye may be the children of your Father which is in heaven; for He maketh His sun to rise on the evil and on the good, and sendeth rain on the just and on the unjust. For if ye love them which love you, what reward have ye? Do not even the publicans the same? And if ye salute your brethren only, what do ye more than others? Do not even the publicans so?" Matt. 5:44-47.

The greatest manifestation of merely human love is to do good to those who do you good. "Greater love hath no man than this, that a man lay down his life for his friends." "But God commendeth His love toward us, in that, while we were yet sinners, Christ died for us." Rom. 5:8. You love your friends, sometimes; but God loves His enemies. That is love itself, because it does not grow out of what He has received from the one He loves. The Savior knew that this kind of love is not possible for your human nature, and so He added these words, "Be ye therefore perfect, even as your Father which is in heaven is perfect." Matt. 5:48. That is, you are to have the perfection of God. Not that you are to become a god, but that you are to allow His life to be manifested in you, and so you will have His perfection. The goodness will all be of God, but will be counted as yours, because you yielded yourself to it, that He might live it in you.

This thought lifts the law of God above the level of mere force, and glorifies it. We "know that His commandment is life everlasting." John 12:50. The Ten Commandments are not arbitrary rules laid down by the Almighty, for the government of people. They are not precepts that exist merely in writing, which you are to read, and then do your best to keep. They are not like the laws of earthly governments, where the lawgivers don't offer the people any help in keeping the laws. God has not given you a law as hard as the stone on which it was traced at Sinai, and then left you to do the best that you can with it, His only concern being to punish you if you come short. It is far different. The law written on tables of stone is but the statement in words of the living righteousness of the living God, which He in love gives to all who will receive it. It is the condition of life, simply because all life comes from God; and since all who will live forever must have His life, it is necessary that they must have His righteousness.

But God has not left you to secure this righteousness by yourself. He well knows that it would be impossible. So He gave Himself, pouring out His own life on the cross, in order that you might have it. So the law of God is the life of God—gracious, loving, and merciful.

One more thought needs to be noted here, and that is, that nothing less than the life of God will meet the demands of the law. Whoever comes short of the glory of God, which is His goodness, is a sinner—a transgressor of the law. The righteousness of God, which is by the faith of Jesus Christ, is the only thing that the law will witness as perfect. Anything less than that will be condemned by the law; for "whatsoever is not of faith is sin." Rom. 14:23. There is no injustice in God's maintaining this high standard for you, since He gives Himself, with all the righteousness of His life, to everyone who will take it. He gives His life freely. All you have to do is to submit yourself to the righteousness of God.

A mere form of godliness will avail nothing. No amount of mere outward conformity to the law will be accepted as the keeping of the law. There is but one God, and so there is but one life of God. He will not acknowledge any rival gods, and He cannot be deceived by a righteousness which is only a counterfeit of His life. Any amount of professed conformity to the law of God, which does not come from the life of God in your soul, is nothing but sin. Don't forget, your righteousness—the keeping of the commandments of God—is only by the faith of Jesus Christ, and that whatsoever is not of faith is sin.

~46~

Weakness and Strength

When you are strong then you are also weak; and you are weak in the very point where your strength is. Were this not so, you would have something of your own to glory in. You are very apt to pride yourself on your "strong points;" but such points are strong only in comparison with other points in your character that are weaker. Compared with the power of the forces of evil, you have no strength, but can manifest only varying degrees of weakness.

It is on these "strong points" that people make their greatest moral failures. Peter's strong point was his boldness; but behold him cowering in the judgment hall, afraid to confess his Lord! Solomon was the wisest man on the earth; but what more pitiable exhibition of folly could there be than the king of Israel surrounded by seven hundred wives and three hundred concubines, listening to their counsel and leading the people of God into idolatry! Moses's strong point was his meekness; but we find him at Meribah saying to the multitude, "Hear now, ye rebels; must we bring you water out of this rock?"

People naturally trust in their "strong" points, and everyone is weak when trusting in themselves. We speak about "guarding our weak points;" but our strong points need guarding just as much. Your weak points include your strong ones. You have nothing but weak points. Whatever point it is that you trust in, that point especially is weak. And you are not guarding the weak points unless you are guarding every point. But you must remember that it is not your resolutions, your will, or your vigilance that guards you, but your faith. "The shield of faith" is what quenches the fiery darts of the wicked. Eph. 6:16. The armor that is prepared for you is not of human manufacture, but is such as God Himself has made in His own wisdom, and endowed with His own strength.

But you need not be discouraged because you find yourself weak where you had fancied yourself strong, for your dependence is not in self, but in God; and depending on Him, you are strong where you are weak. This was the experience of Paul, as he wrote to the Corinthians. 2 Cor. 12:10. You only need to unite your weakness to God's strength. Then, like the apostle, you can "take pleasure in infirmities, and reproaches, in necessities, in persecutions, in distresses, for Christ's sake."

God has to reveal your weakness to you before He can save you. The devil, on the other hand, leads you to think you are strong in order that, by trusting in yourself, you may fall and be ruined. When you feel strong, the admonition is, "Let him that thinketh he standeth take heed lest he fall." 1 Cor. 10:12. But when you feel weak, too weak to do anything of yourself, you are in a position to gain the victory. The danger is that you will not feel weak enough; for even in your weakest moments you have strength enough to resist the Holy Spirit and prevent God from working in your life. If you are weak enough to yield entirely to the Lord, then for those purposes for which you need strength, you become as strong as the Lord Himself, for you have His strength.

~47~

Christian Growth

Growth is the process of development by which the immature advances toward a state of perfection. Growth is as much a possibility and a necessity of spiritual life as of physical life. The spiritual life begins with birth—the "new birth." You are then a babe in Christ. If you remain a babe then you cannot become a soldier of the cross, enduring hardness in the service of your Master. You can't partake of the strong meat which, with the more simple "milk of the word," is provided in the Gospel of Christ. From the condition of a babe, you must pass to that of the full stature of a man or woman in Christ; and this can only be done by growth.

What are the essentials to growth? Almost anyone can tell what is necessary to the growth of a plant, but scarcely anyone seems to understand what is necessary to development as a Christian. Yet it needs no greater effort to know what is necessary in the one case than in the other. A Christian is but a plant in the garden of the Lord; and spiritual plants, like any other plants, need plenty of water, good soil, and sunlight.

The Lord has provided all of these for His garden, and it only remains for His plants to assimilate what they find. But there is a strange perversity about these human plants that is not seen in the physical world. The Lord complains to the prophet Jeremiah about His people of old, that though He had planted them "a noble vine, wholly a right seed," yet they had "turned into the degenerate plant of a strange vine;" and it is that way with many now who have enjoyed similar privileges. There is no fault in the provision that God has made; but there is an evil principle that finds its way into the plant and perverts its nature, causing degeneracy and ultimately the loss of all that is noble and good.

It is the nature of a plant to turn towards the sun; but in God's spiritual garden some plants try to grow in another way. There are some that try to grow by something inherent in themselves. Of course, no growth can be attained in this way. Imagine a plant trying to make itself grow, exerting itself—if it could be capable of exertion—to become higher and stronger and to strike its roots more deeply into the soil! The idea is absurd; yet this is what many people think they must do in order to grow as Christians. But Christ said, "which of you with taking thought can add to his stature one cubit?" Luke 12:25. Who would think of exerting himself in order to grow physically?

It is true that exercise influences growth, but it is not the cause of growth, and there isn't anything that you can do to cause it. The principle of development is in every person by nature; and all that you can do is to secure those conditions so that this principle can operate. So it is in the spiritual world. The principle of growth is implanted by God at the new birth, and only needs right conditions to cause the babe in Christ to grow up to the full stature of Christian maturity. You can interfere with this principle, and repress it, but you cannot create it. But the devil, who understands all this, continually sets people to work to try to make themselves grow by exertion. He would have you think that by taking thought and doing a large amount of good works you can add a cubit to your stature in Christ. And people try this plan, as they have been doing for ages in the past, and keep trying it until they find that it does not work. They find that after years of such efforts, they are not any stronger Christians than they were at the start, nor do they reach higher up into the spiritual atmosphere of heaven. Then they become discouraged, and the devil, who knew what the result would be, comes and tempts them, and finds them ready to fall an easy prey to his devices.

But there is no impossibility in the way of Christian growth. The difficulty was, you did not understand the nature of that growth. You did not know the conditions under which alone it could take place. You were not instructed by that which God has revealed in His word and in nature. A plant grows and reaches up and becomes stronger without any exertion on its own part. It simply looks to the sun. It feels the vivifying influence of its rays, and reaches up toward the source from which they come. The whole process is simply an effort to get nearer to the source of its life. In the soil it finds water and the various elements that enter into its composition as a plant, and the principle of assimilation within it, which it has, so long as it looks at the sun, draws up the substances through the roots and into the stem and leaves. The plant simply lets the process go on according to this law of assimilation which its Creator gave it.

So it must be with the plants in the heavenly garden. They must look at the sun. You cannot grow by looking at yourself; you cannot grow by looking at other plants around you. Neither should you exert yourself to assimilate what is necessary to build you up and make you strong, but simply let the process of assimilation go on according to the "law of the Spirit of life" that has been put within you. "Let this mind be in you, which was also in Christ Jesus," is the exhortation that is given you. It will be in you if you will let it. All God wants of you is to let Him work in you.

People are continually doing something to hinder God's work. They are continually putting self in God's way. They refuse to submit their will to God's will. And this is all the difficulty in living the Christian life. It is not a difficulty of performing works, but the difficulty of making the right choice, of yielding to God and not to self, of looking to Christ and not to something else, and of letting His mind and His spirit be in you. He is your Sun, the "Sun of Righteousness." Mal. 4:2. If you will look steadfastly at Him as the plant looks at the sun that shines in the heavens; if you will make it your constant effort to turn toward Him as the plant turns to the source of its life, and to reach up more and more toward the brightness of His face, then you will experience no difficulty in obtaining the full measure of growth that you desire.

But you need not expect to realize the fact that you are growing, any more than you can realize that you are growing physically by trying to note changes in your height from day to day. If the plant turns its head away from the sun to look at itself to see how fast it is growing, it will soon cease to grow; and just so with the Christian. When you try to see yourself growing spiritually you are taking one of the most effective means to stop your growth entirely.

So there is no cause for discouragement in the fact you don't at any time realize this process of growth. It is taking place just as truly as it takes place in the physical world, and you don't need to make the outcome a matter of anxious concern. The outcome will be what the Apostle Paul describes in his letter to the Ephesians, for whom he prayed that they might be strengthened by the inward presence of the Spirit, "that ye, being rooted and grounded in love, may be able to comprehend with all saints what is the length and breadth and depth and height, and to know the love of Christ, which passeth knowledge, that ye might be filled with all the fullness of God." Eph. 3:17-19.

You are not told to grow in the knowledge of self or the knowledge of your sinfulness or that of your neighbors, but "in grace, and in the knowledge of our Lord and Savior Jesus Christ." 2 Pet. 3:18. You cannot know His grace and all His attributes unless you see them; and you cannot see them unless you look to Him.

~48~

The Judgment

Felix, himself Paul's judge, trembled as the apostle preached to him of "righteousness, temperance, and judgment to come." Just for a moment the doctrine of the judgment was pressed so closely home to his calloused senses that he trembled as he thought of appearing himself before the Judge of all.

You may take a live coal from the fire and by handling it lightly, toss it from hand to hand without scorching your fingers. But if you firmly grasp it then it burns its way into your flesh. Multitudes hold the doctrine of the judgment so lightly that it has little effect on their daily lives. In a general way they believe in a day of reckoning, but it is not held firmly enough to burn its way into the heart and life.

You readily comprehend the truth that the world will be judged. You may even feel the satisfaction which the Psalmist expressed when he saw that evil would not always triumph, and that workers of iniquity would not be able to corrupt judgment in the day of God. But your thoughts must bring the matter nearer to yourself than that.

"Every one of us shall give account of himself to God." Not merely the world in general and not solely the wicked who have lived in wantonness, but "every one of us." Not as a church member, or in your family, but singly and alone you will meet the account that is kept in heaven's books. What will other people say? Does that make a difference to you? Are you afraid to follow the Lord because of the reproach of Christ? Of what value is the record the world may write when the books of heaven are recording the story of your life?

Your life is made up of three things—deeds, words, and thoughts.

1. *Your Deeds.*—God "will render to every man according to his deeds." Rom. 2:6. Don't deceive yourself by what you profess. "He that doeth righteousness is righteous." The apostle writes of those who "profess that they know God; but in works they deny Him." Titus 1:16. Not what you profess, but your deeds determine your destiny.

2. *Your Words.*—"But I say unto you, That every idle word that men shall speak, they shall give account thereof in the day of judgment." Matt. 12:36. "Out of the abundance of the heart the mouth speaketh." Therefore it is fair that your life should be judged by your words. Foolish frivolity in your heart will manifest itself in lightness of speech. Vanity within flows forth in "great swelling words of vanity." Hatred of God's law and lawlessness within your heart will lead to words against the Divine standard of righteousness. When you realize that even your offhand and idle words—and especially the words uttered with determination and forethought—are recorded, you may well pray the Psalmist's prayer: "Set a watch, O LORD, before my mouth; keep the door of my lips."

3. *Your Thoughts.*—Your deeds and words are seen and heard by others, and may be controlled so that the true condition of your heart is not always revealed. But the judgment will not be according to the world's standards. "He said unto them, Ye are they which justify yourselves before men; but God knoweth your hearts: for that which is highly esteemed among men is abomination in the sight of God." Luke 16:15. "For the word of God is quick, and powerful, and sharper than any two-edged sword, piercing even to the dividing asunder of soul and spirit, and of the joints and marrow, and is a discerner of the thoughts and intents of the heart. Neither is there any creature that is not manifest in His sight: but all things are naked and opened unto the eyes of Him with whom we have to do." Heb. 4:12, 13.

The law of God is spiritual, and by it every secret sin will be revealed. "Let us hear the conclusion of the whole matter: Fear God, and keep His commandments; for this is the whole duty of man. For God shall bring every work into judgment, with every secret thing, whether it be good, or whether it be evil." Eccl. 12:13, 14.

The whole aim of the Gospel is to teach you how the righteousness of the holy and perfect law may be fulfilled in you—by Jesus Christ the righteous One. The judgment will reveal all your works of self, and blessed are you whose transgression is forgiven, whose sin is covered in that day. Since it is the law of God that is to be the standard of judgment, it isn't strange that Satan should seek to lead you to despise the law, and to continue in sin. Lawlessness is a special mark of the last days in prophecy. In the same last days, when the "hour of His judgment is come," you won't be surprised that the message of the Gospel is in a special sense a call to loyalty and obedience.

When you are brought face to face with the judgment you cannot afford to treat with contempt the law which places you under sin. Now, when not only in the professedly godless world are people rushing on in sin, but when even in the pulpits and the religious world the law of God is being treated as an outward thing, the time has come that the Gospel calls in a "loud voice," "Fear God, and give glory to Him; for the hour of His judgment is come." Rev. 14:7.

~49~

The Final Cleansing

Before the close of His earthly ministry the Lord cleansed the temple; so before He closes His heavenly ministry and comes to take His own, He cleanses His temple—the church—that it may meet Him without deceit at His coming.

"But who may abide the day of His coming? and who shall stand when He appeareth? for He is like a refiner's fire, and like fullers' soap; and He shall sit as a refiner and purifier of silver: and He shall purify the sons of Levi, and purge them as gold and silver, that they may offer unto the LORD an offering in righteousness." Mal. 3:2, 3.

Revelation 18 shows the desperate condition of the religious world just before the Lord comes, and the call from God is, "Come out of her, My people." It is a call to you to reform your life, to forsake sin and self, and to take the salvation of God.

It is by the Word that you are cleansed from sin (John 15:3) and that the Gospel is preached (1 Pet. 1:25). In Rev. 14:6-14 the Lord has given an outline of the message that is to go to every person, with the power to cleanse you so you can be a living stone in the living temple of God. It is the work that you should now be engaged in, for the day of the Lord is surely at hand, and His Word is to be set before you to prepare you to abide the day of His coming.

"Blow ye the trumpet in Zion, and sound an alarm in My holy mountain; let all the inhabitants of the land tremble: for the day of the LORD cometh, for it is nigh at hand." Joel 2:1. "Be ye clean that bear the vessels of the LORD." Isa. 52:11.

Notes

References

Legend:

W   E. J. Waggoner
J   A. T. Jones

PT   The Present Truth
ST   The Signs of the Times
RH   The Advent Review and Sabbath Herald
BE   The Bible Echo